The Success Guide for Home Services
Follow a Proven Path to Profit, Wealth, & Freedom

What is a big advantage of this book?

- Structure your operations for profitability
- Earn what you need and deserve
- Your employees make the money they need
- Give your customers what they really want
- Build a business that is sustainable and sellable

The Success Guide packs two years of Business School for Owners into an easy-to-understand handbook.

Copyright © 2024 by Peak Leadership.

This easy-to-read book is filled with stories, examples, and tools for business owners. This is a "must-read" for every service business owner. These concepts work in heating, cooling, plumbing, roofing, electrical, and most retail home services.

ISBN: 9798346298045

Foreword

In a world where the demands of the service industry continue to evolve, The Success Guide for Home Services serves as a crucial resource for contractors seeking to thrive in this competitive landscape.

This guidebook distills two years of Business School into practical, actionable insights tailored specifically for the unique challenges of service contractors. It doesn't just present theory; it lays out a proven path toward building a successful, sustainable, and sellable business.

The power of this book lies in its ability to simplify complex processes. It empowers you to take charge of your profitability and earn what you truly deserve. By focusing on what both your employees and customers need, you create an environment where everyone can thrive.

I encourage you to read one chapter a day. Then think about ways to apply the concepts for a more effective business. This guidebook offers you the tools to not only navigate your business intricacies but to master them. By implementing its principles, you can transform operations and build a legacy that stands the test of time. Remember -

Positive change creates positive results.

I know The Success Guide for Home Services will serve as a trusted resource on your path to a more profitable and fulfilling future.

Kerry S. Webb, PhD, CCO
Peak Leadership Consulting
November 2024

TABLE OF CONTENTS

Chapter 1 - Build a Healthy Business   p. 7
- What makes a Healthy Business?
- Organizational Health Check
- Business Doctor
- Business Basics

Chapter 2 - Creating Culture   p. 15
- Core values
- Mission, Vision
  Energy & Motivation
- Performance & Results

Chapter 3 - Staffing Your Team   p. 31
- Techs
- Install team
- Office
  - CSRs
  - Dispatch
  - Bookkeeping

Chapter 4 - Hiring Done Right   p. 39
- Recruiting & Interviewing
- Testing & Onboarding

Chapter 5 - Firing Effectively   p. 51
- Gut Feelings
- Pre-Firing Practices or Termination Avoidance Strategies
- Termination Process
- Replacement

TABLE OF CONTENTS

Chapter 6 - Compensation that Works   p. 57
- Incentives and Motivation
- Performance
- Spiffs are Dead
- Pay for the Results you Want
- Put Compensation in your Employee's Hands

Chapter 7 - Coaching for Success   p. 61
- Behaviors are 1st
- Time management is 2nd
- Energy and Focus Matter more than Time
- Core Values are the Inner Guide
- Training

Chapter 8 - Reaching Top Performance   p. 69
- Tech Performance
- Installer Performance
- Sales Team Performance
- CSR Performance
- Dispatch Performance
- Bookkeeper Performance
- Business Performance

Chapter 9 - Get Your Pricing Right   p. 79
- How do you price?
- How often should you raise prices?
- How much should you mark up your service?
- How much should you mark up your equipment?
- What should you pay for installation?

TABLE OF CONTENTS

Chapter 10 - Plan Your Profits   p. 91
- True Breakeven
- What is a reasonable Cost of Goods Sold?
- What is an acceptable Gross Profit?
- What is a good target for Operations/Expenses??

Chapter 11 - Build a Team of Rock Stars   p. 101
- Your Service Team
- Your Sales and Install Team
- Your Office Team
- Your Management Team

Chapter 12 - Sustained Business Growth   p. 111
- What is an easy and successful way to plan business growth?
- How do you build a process to achieve your goals?
- Build a Recession Proof Business

How To Use This Book:

I encourage you to read this book slowly and take your time. It is probably best to read only one chapter a day. Then take time to think about ways you can apply the concepts and tools for a more effective business.

The Success Guide is written for owners of home service businesses, managers in home service businesses, and employees in home services. Most anyone who reads this book will discover "life truths" that result in greater income, wealth, and freedom. If this book has a positive impact on your life, won't you consider some friend or coworkers to share a copy with?

Use this guidebook to transform your business, your teams, and yourself. Many readers find they benefit even more the second time the read the book than the first time.

REMEMBER -

Positive change creates positive results.

Chapter 1
BUILDING A HEALTHY BUSINESS

Do you own a healthy business or does your business "own" you? What I am really asking is "Does your business produce the results you need or not?

Does your business feel like a never-ending job? Does it sometimes seem as if you are running on a hamster wheel? You may be running as fast as you can, but as best you can tell, you are not getting anywhere.

Why does it seem so hard to build a healthy business? More often than I would like, business owners tell me they feel like they own a job rather than feeling a sense of freedom.

Their business demands constant attention. They feel if they take their eye off the ball for even a couple of days, then things will deteriorate and begin to slide downhill. This may feel like reality for these business owners, but it is certainly not "TRUTH" for an owner with the right plan to execute.

When I talk with owners who own a healthy business, we mostly talk about the goals achieved, their recent travels, and their plans for an even brighter future. A healthy business should provide you with MORE freedom, MORE wealth, and MORE profitability.

You see, some people think that cooking is difficult. The truth is cooking is simple…if you follow a good recipe, have the right tools, and use good equipment, then you stand a good chance of a great outcome.

Cooking begins with following a basic set of instructions. You have to learn the principles of the kitchen. Put the most used utensils where you can get to them easily. Immediately wash and clean the pots, pans, and trays that you use most often. Dry everything well and take good care of your cooking tools.

Learn how to measure ingredients and know the number of ounces in a cup, pint, quart, etc. Have a timer and use it religiously.

Cooking is about finding a good set of instructions (we call it a recipe) and then following the recipe carefully. Building a healthy business is the same. If you do not have a solid recipe for a healthy business, then it is no surprise that you often get "burned".

I remember the first time I cooked a pot of fresh peas. I had grown them in my backyard garden. I watered and cared for them for weeks. When the pea pods began to grow, I would carefully pick the biggest and most plump ones each day and then take them inside for a quick rinse. Then I shelled the pods and stored the peas in plastic storage bags in the refrigerator until the bags were full. When I had my first full bag of peas, I could hardly wait to cook them.

I called my mom to learn how she cooked peas and to ask her to share her recipe with me. She told me the steps that she followed. I listened carefully – but I DID NOT WRITE ANYTHING DOWN. Big mistake!

Obtain a good recipe for growth and follow it.

I rinsed the peas again and put them in some water to boil. Then I added some salt and pepper without measuring. How hard could this be really? I threw in a couple pieces of bacon as she recommended, and I waited for the peas to cook. After 50 minutes or so, I did a taste test. The peas were still a tiny bit harder than I liked, so I cooked them another 10 minutes.

Now a second taste test. The consistency was perfect. But the taste was blah. They didn't taste bad. They just did not have much flavor at all. The peas tasted nothing like I remembered from enjoying my mom's peas.

I called Mom again and asked her to read the recipe to me while I took notes. Once again, she patiently explained step-by-step how to prepare the peas.

This time, I noticed that she mentioned using chicken broth as a base. I didn't remember that from before. I had just used plain water. She also mentioned cooking the bacon in a pan by itself until it was almost brown and chopping it up before putting it into the pot with the peas. Had she mentioned this before?

I could not remember. One other item that she mentioned stands out as well…cut up a small onion and add it to the peas after browning the onions in the bacon grease. What???

Now I know I would have remembered this if she had mentioned it to me in our previous conversation. I asked her if she had referred to her recipe when I first asked her about cooking peas, and she told me that she had not looked at the recipe when we talked the first time. She thought I probably just needed some basic instructions, and she did not want to overwhelm or confuse me.

The results of my not taking careful notes and not having the full set of her instructions to follow were distasteful. In fact, the peas had so little flavor that I threw them out.

However, after asking Mom to share the details for her recipe and my taking careful notes and asking questions, my second pot of peas were delicious. They were so good that I could barely stop eating them.

What made the difference? It is critical to have a complete set of instructions and to follow the recipe step-by-step.

Take action step-by-step.

What Makes a Business Healthy?

How do you rate the health of your business? Here are a few questions to ask to get a baseline on the health of your business.

1) If you were to not show up at work for the next week, would your business produce the same average revenues as when you are at work every day?

2) When you are around your employees, do you hear a good bit of laughter and good-natured joking?

3) Is your annual net profit before taxes, higher than 10%?

4) Do employees that you consider to be above average or excellent make more money each year?

5) Is the owner paying himself or herself a reasonable salary each month from the business?

6) Does the business have "cash in the bank" to sustain payroll for 60-90 days or more in the event of a major crisis or slow work season?

7) Do your employees show up for work at least 5-10 minutes before the workday begins?

8) Do your managers agree that positive energy is practiced by most of your employees?

Organizational Health Check

Unless you can answer positively to at least 5 of these 8 questions, your business likely needs to undergo an organizational health check. If your business is not healthy, then no amount of time, effort or energy that you pour into a business is going to achieve the results that you desire. It is like cooking your peas longer to make them taste better without adding the proper ingredients. It simply will not work.

An organizational health check is a fast and easy way to get feedback from everyone in your company. It only takes a few minutes for each employee to respond, and the results are confidential. This will give you feedback that is quite informative and greatly beneficial. You MUST be willing to hear the feedback with a mindset to improve and not take it personally. The truth is the truth. What you do about it is what matters.

Over the years, I have helped many business owners walk away from their daily duties in the business and create a "life schedule" that is more balanced, fun, and healthy for their family. A healthy business should NOT own your time.

Complete an organizational health check.

If this is your personal experience, then your business needs to undergo an Organizational Health Check. You need to find out where your business is "ill" or "unhealthy" if you want more freedom. Only then can you put the correct strategies in place to get your business on the road to recovery for financial and emotional health.

A Business Coach

What is a business coach? A business coach is like a physician who helps owners and general managers identify areas where their business is unhealthy and/or underperforming.

I work with a team of business coaches, and we train, coach, and consult with business owners. Together we collaborate and implement strategies to bring over 200 businesses into a healthy, profitable status every month.

The results of our efforts are impressive. This past year, we reviewed the business growth of our clients and compared it to the amount they paid us in fees. The average return on investment was more than 28 times what our clients paid for our services. This is a 2800% ROI!

Over the years, I have worked with hundreds of businesses including medical and dental surgery groups, accounting and engineering firms, Fortune 500 companies, and many, many small businesses that interface directly with customers.

Hands down my favorite companies to work with are service contractors. These personally owned businesses are classified by the U.S. Small Business Administration as small businesses because they have fewer than 500 employees (IRS.gov, 2019).

My personal definition of a small business is a company with fewer than 100 employees and average revenues under $50 million. My favorite clients are those with less than 50 team members and annual revenues of $3 to $10 million. With a solid growth strategy and weekly accountability, these companies typically double in size within 2 years or less and then double in size again just as quickly.

Most of the companies we work with range from $2 million up to $20 million in revenues with 15 - 75 employees. I have worked with plenty of companies that are larger and a few that are smaller, but this description fits 80% to 85% of the businesses that we work with.

Why do we focus on this segment of businesses? It is simple. These businesses are small enough to implement changes without tons of bureaucracy, yet large enough to take good care of their employees. The owners are authentic enough to admit their weaknesses and be responsive to solid coaching. These organizations are prone to listen, adapt, and experience the benefits of coaching and consulting quickly.

In short, this describes many residential and retail service companies. Most of these business owners lack the super-inflated egos of some corporate leaders. Small business owners realize they are not the only reason for their business success. Their achievement depends on building a successful team who cooperate and work together.

Small business owners are also thankful for the value and insights provided by a business coach. The owners listen with a desire to improve and change, rather than defend their prior decisions. Small businesses are less mired in bureaucracy. They are willing to change their processes and try new methods as long as they see results.

Smart owners change methods to get better results.

Some leaders in larger organizations (but not all) have egos that are out of control. They will not admit it. They do not see it. They think they are better at leading than what their employees are experiencing and know to be true. When a person sits at the top of a large business, it is easy to think he or she deserves the credit for the business's success.

The truth is the credit for great success almost always goes to the team of employees who flex, improvise, and figure out how to keep customers happy. At the same time, good employees strive to implement instructions from management which may press against the goal of keeping customers or making customers happy.

You see, employees usually "see" and know the "true reality" about the health of your work environment. In smaller businesses, it is harder to hide the flaws. When an owner is willing to accept the need to improve personally, it becomes much easier to talk about the shortcomings of their business departments, managers, and employees and this helps them to experience improvements more quickly.

Business Basics

1) First, you need a healthy culture and core values that generate commitment, not compliance from employees and customers.

14

2) Second, you must have sustainable processes that deliver consistent results and are not difficult to follow.

3) Third, you need employees who respect each other and the work they do, who care about your customers, and who strive to do a good job every day.

These three factors are present in ALL healthy businesses. Believe it or not, most businesses that are unhealthy are not suffering from a bad pool of employees. Now there may be one or two employees that need to go, but by far the majority of employees come to work each day wanting to do a good job.

Business is a game.

Most often it is your business systems and processes that are creating poor results and unwanted behaviors. You see, employees "play" the game of business by the rules that exist. If you want different results, then you need to create different rules to work by.

Employees learn to play by the rules of your business.

I have seen more businesses succeed by changing the ways they compensate and reward employees, than by increasing salaries and hourly wages. It is more important to spend time motivating employees, than to double down on eliminating mistakes and wasted effort or resources. Most people already want to do a good job. Encourage the right behavior and the wrong behavior will be replaced or eliminated.

Good systems make it easy for employees to do the right thing for your customers. Bad systems make it easy for an employee with a wrong motive or bad attitude to do the wrong thing to a customer.

Often, it is the business systems or processes that stand in the way of your success. Up to 80% of the time it is the system that failed and not the employee when things go wrong with a customer experience. Most people are trying to do the right thing and they intend to do a good job.

Good systems create positive results!

One of the first steps to take in evaluating your systems is to read your customer reviews and find out how your systems are impacting the people who keep you in business.

Review customer comments. What are they are telling you?

As an owner, you may be so close to the situation AND because the business can feel like an extension of yourself, it can be difficult for you to see the problems that exist or to grasp how easily things can be remedied. Owners tend to blame employees first and later consider the impact of their systems. It should be the other way around.

Most people want to do a good job.

Takeaways from this chapter.

- *Obtain a good recipe for growth and follow it.*

- *Take action step-by-step.*

- *Smart owners change methods to get better results.*

- *Business is a game.*

- *Employees learn to play by the rules of your business.*

- *Good systems create positive results!*

- *Most people want to do a good job.*

Chapter 2
CREATING A POSITIVE WORK CULTURE

What is the general mood that I would observe if I showed up at your company tomorrow? How do employees seem to feel and behave when they come into work daily?

- Are people laughing and joking with one another? Or do employees seem stressed or depressed?

- How do they feel when thinking about going in to work on Monday morning? Are they tired or enthusiastic?

- Does going to work represent an opportunity or a hassle?

- Does your business feel more like a struggle, or does it feel like an endless source of income and success?

I work with business owners almost every single day. They come in all shapes, sizes, ages, and personalities. I can tell you that I look forward to working with most of them. Most days I can hardly wait for our training sessions to start.

Healthy business owners and general managers have good personal energy. They are optimistic about their business potential, and they view challenges as an opportunity to improve. We laugh and joke with one another. We also discuss tough issues.

The energy and mood of these owners and managers is also contagious. The employees pick up on this mood and they reflect and replicate the owner's overall attitude and behavior.

Through our conversations, these owners are open to press in on uncomfortable topics and areas of underperformance. This allows us to make improvements and implement changes. For these owners, business is like a tool or a game that provides opportunities, challenges, and sometimes fun. Does this sound like your situation?

Other owners and general managers are less exciting to coach. They tend to procrastinate on their progress reports and KPIs (Key Performance Indicators). They are quick to recount the week's challenges and problems with technicians and customers. Rather than focusing on a single issue and resolving it, they jump from one problem to another in the conversation. This is not constructive, and the result is like pouring gasoline on the fires in their business.

They stay amped up about mistakes, failures, and misunderstandings. We do not spend much time on laughter because they view life and business as "serious topics". They would probably not admit it, but they view the glass as half full. Remember this – We tend to attract more of whatever we focus on.

Individual truth is very personal. For owners, their business feels like an extension of their own life. They focus on the problems, failures, and shortcomings of their team. They are quick to point out that it is difficult to find good people, customers are unreasonable, costs are too high, and on and on. Does this ever sound like you?

Do you want more wins or more fires? You will get more of whatever you choose to focus on.

Focus on wins and attract more positive results.

You see, much of the time we create our own reality. Our life is very much a reflection of how we view the world around us. People treat us as we view them. As I said earlier, our thoughts and energy are contagious. We tend to attract exactly what we are thinking. This might sound a little "out there" for some of you but remember that our thoughts have energy and a frequency of their own. What are you projecting?

Our thoughts and energy are contagious.

Have you ever known someone that you didn't like and maybe even felt was a jerk? Of course, you have. However, maybe someone else that you respect and like, saw this person very differently? Maybe this other person even got along with the "jerk" and actually seemed to like them. How is this possible?

It might seem crazy that someone else could value the same person that you perceive as a pain in the ass. Just the same, many of us have experienced this unique phenomenon. How can this happen?

Well, it comes down to the way we view the other person. While you saw their flaws and failures, your friend most likely saw their strengths and value. You see WE ALL HAVE FLAWS AND WEAKNESSES.

The way that someone treats me certainly affects the way that I feel about them. Most likely, it impacts the way I respond to them. My body language will also reflect the way I feel about them.

In fact, many times we know whether someone likes us or is upset with us, without the other person speaking a word. Usually, when the boss walks by without speaking to us, we get a very strong message regarding our value and importance to our boss…and the message is NOT good.

We all have flaws and weaknesses.

If I have a good feeling about the person, I am more likely to smile around them and to engage in conversation. If I do not have a good feeling about the other person, it is likely that I will avoid them and probably not attempt to engage in or have any sustained conversation with them unless it is unavoidable. Even then, our conversation will likely remain more serious in tone with little laughter or humor thrown in.

- How do you think your employees feel about **you**?
- More importantly, "How do employees think **you** feel about them"?

You see, a long time ago I learned that people perceive what you think of them whether you tell them or not. Your eyes and your body language give it away. Other people sense if you are critical or negative about them. They observe whether you see them as "valuable" or "important". They know whether you tend to see the flaws in others more than you notice their strengths.

In business, the owner and general manager are the PRIMARY drivers of work environment and the company culture. You CANNOT change the company culture just by having two or three company "outings" or social events each year. Gatherings support the retention of a good culture, but gatherings and company outings will NOT create a good culture.

Culture is created daily. You change the company culture by coming to work with a smile in your heart and on your face. This brings positive energy into the workplace, and you pass on this energy to every employee that you encounter.

Good managers bring positive energy into the workplace.

What if your employees are afraid of you or avoid you? I promise this kind of energy and negative feeling will most definitely prevent your business from achieving double digit net profits. People are drawn toward doing their best when they believe their leader believes the best about them.

Culture is created daily.

Some people are so caught up in "collecting hurts" that they are unable and unwilling to give their best. These people need assistance and awareness of their need to forgive and let go. Until they let go of life's hurts, they will remain mediocre, overly sensitive, and unhappy.

However, don't let these few people skew your view of humanity. Most employees try to do a good job. Most people really want to feel that they achieved something worthwhile at work. Very few folks are looking to just "do time" and get through 40 hours a week just to collect their pay.

If you believe that is the way people see the workplace, it will certainly affect the way you treat them, which will certainly affect the way they see your workplace. People respond to the attitude and energy of their supervisor.

Do you see how this is a cycle? So, who owns the final result? You do…the business owner. You are the leader. It is your business.

People respond to the attitude & energy of their supervisor.

Your work culture is developed just like a happy marriage is developed. Work culture reflects the health of the relationships in the workplace. Just as a happy marriage is built day after day by treating our spouse with kindness, respect, and appreciation, the same behaviors are needed in the workplace.

As a spouse you must be committed every day to focus on the good things about your spouse. Why did you choose them? What attracted you? Be thankful for these traits daily.

Accept the fact that your spouse has faults, and you need to overlook their shortcomings or else, you should step in and offer your support and help. A good marriage is designed to bring balance to our life.

This is the reason for most of us, that our spouse is our opposite in many ways. If they were just like us, then how would this bring balance into our lives?

Our spouse is not weaker or inferior to us. Their strengths are usually not our strengths. As opposites, we were attracted to each other and by focusing on the other person's natural strengths and abilities, we continue to affirm them. In turn, our spouse feels valued and naturally feels the same way toward us.

However, in some relationships, couples turn their opposites into criticisms. It is true that opposites attract and equally true that some opposites can attack! The person who is your opposite can be a great source of balance and perspective if you model respect and appreciation. They are not your enemy.

People who are your opposite are not your enemy.

Let me tell you a story that happened to me. Several years ago, I found myself traveling a lot and as a result, I experienced a period where I had very little time with my wife. When I was at home, I was often playing "catch up" on the work that didn't get done while I was out of town. As a result, she felt alone and neglected.

Now I didn't do this on purpose. I was just doing my best to be a good employee and to provide for my family. However, as I was teaching a training session on leadership, it dawned on me that I was not implementing this principle of positive attitude transfer in my own marriage.

At the break, I pulled out my daily agenda journal and added a new item to my list – "Give my wife at least three honest compliments a day". That night after the training was finished, I made sure to compliment something I really liked about her on our evening phone call. (There are usually a LOT of things that we like about our spouse and of course a few things we wish were different.) What do you focus on when you think about your spouse? If you think mostly about the things, you really like about them, you are more likely to have a happy and positive relationship.

Positive energy transfer improves most relationships.

I believe my wife was appreciative of my compliment, but she didn't seem to react any differently. The next day when I got home, I told her that I missed her and thought of three good compliments which I delivered throughout the day. That evening, as I was getting ready for bed, I gave her another small compliment. To my surprise, she stopped me in my tracks with her next statement.

She said, "You have started doing something recently that you haven't done for a while. I haven't figured out what it is yet, but I really like it. Keep doing it!"

The positive energy transfer worked! What she was feeling was the positive emotion of being valued and esteemed. My failure to show her the appreciation she deserved had left her feeling empty and alone, as I was often away during this period. During the rest of this travel period, she remained positive and told me how much she looked forward to our evening phone calls. When I was home, you can imagine how much more we enjoyed our time together.

Life is too short if you value the right things. Life is too long if you value the wrong things. The true purpose of living is to build healthy, positive relationships based on love. Wow! Did you hear that?

The purpose of life is to build positive relationships.

So how do I define love? Love is NOT a feeling. Love is really an issue of respect. It is treating people the way they NEED to be treated, NOT the way they deserve to be treated. It means being patient with someone when you are frustrated or feeling impatient. It means talking to others in a tactful and respectful manner, even if they are being disrespectful or behaving in a way that is unacceptable. Love is how we act. Love is not always how we feel.

Love is an action, not a feeling.

Core Values

What are your core values? Where did you get them? How do you live them? Why do you believe your core values are the correct way to live?

Good questions, huh? We have to think about how we live if we are going to live a good life.

For over 20 years I have been a business coach and at the same time a full-time business professor serving as a management professor at a university in the Dallas metro area. In class, I have a practice of asking my students (especially in morning classes) to rate their day by a show of hands on a scale of 1 to 10 fingers. Showing less than five fingers means the day is off to a rough start and 9 or 10 fingers means they are having a good or a great day.

I am often surprised by the number of college students who only raise two or three fingers. I explain to them that the way they rate their day on a regular basis is most likely the way they will rate their life as they look back at it 40 years from now.

You see, we are people of habit. When we get into a habit of having days that are rated at a 1 or 2, before we know it our entire life has been a string of days that are only a 1 or 2. If you are in the habit of getting your mental outlook to a 9 or 10 before you leave your house for work, then you will begin to string together more years and more days that are rated as a 9 or 10. Isn't that the kind of life you want to experience? The simple practice of thinking about your daily outlook can change your life.

Now do I wake up every day feeling like a 9 or 10 when my alarm sounds at 4:45 am? LOL. Not usually. At that early hour of the day, my body is usually moving slowly, and my back is usually tight and stiff after several back surgeries.

So, I turn on the lights to get some positive energy flowing. Light gives us energy. Then I take a hot shower, shave, and get dressed. Then I make my morning coffee. I also like to listen to inspiring music. By the time I am dressed, my goal is to be at a 10 every morning well before I see my first client.

My days tend to start at 5:00 am because I live in Texas and many of my clients are on the east coast. This means that by the time I shower, shave, and get dressed, it is already 7:00 am and time to get to work, even though it will only be 6:00 am (CST) in Texas. When I turn on the camera for our video training sessions, I want to exude energy, enthusiasm, and to remind my clients that I like them, and they are important to me.

My clients are not paying me to be tired and sluggish when I start my 6:00 am coaching sessions. I am usually more energetic than my clients for the 6:00 am sessions even though they are in the eastern time zone, where it is 7:00 am for them.

They have already been awake an hour longer than me! So how can I have more energy than they do? Some of them do not have a goal of living every day as a 10!

We create the life we want. Smart people don't just hope it happens. Smart people create the life they want.

My parents taught me values through conversations, at times with corrective discipline, and by living the way they expected my sister and me to live. My grandparents also played a major role in defining my core values, probably as much as my parents. They modeled joy and love (and discipline) every time we were around them. As a result, we truly looked forward to seeing our grandparents. Yes, they spoiled us, but they also had clear expectations for how we acted and how we treated people.

Smart people create the life they want.

One of my grandfathers was Emerson Webb. He was a small man who stood at 5 feet and 6 inches tall. However, he was physically strong and was possibly the most patient person I have ever known. His patience served him well as a grandfather to some highly energetic grandkids, but also as the husband to my grandmother. My grandmother was named Jimmy Lea, and she was a passionate woman, but not always easy to be around.

She loved us grandkids with all her heart. She spoiled us and let us get away with more than we should have. At the same time, she was easily worked up about things. I remember so many times when she would yell out my grandfather's name when we got out of line. "Emerson, do something about these kids", she would yell.

For some unknown reason, it seemed to be papaw Emerson's job to straighten us out and to get us to follow the rules. He would stop whatever he was doing and patiently explain to us what we were doing that was not acceptable. Then he would tell us to "be good now and not upset Jimmy Lea anymore."

Most of the time, we didn't even feel like we were reprimanded. We were just trying to not have grandmother get upset and holler at papaw Emerson. We all wanted to please our papaw.

People try to please when they respect or admire you.

When driving in their car, my grandmother was a "passenger side driver". This was another experience in itself. I do not know how my grandfather continued to be so patient on road trips. My grandmother's continual critique of my grandfather's driving created stress for me. I do not know how he remained so calm with her, except that he loved my grandmother deeply. My grandfather saw her strengths and valued her deeply.

My father was the youngest of three brothers. His oldest two brothers were twins, and they were 12 years older than my father. It took me a while to figure it out, but evidently my father was a surprise baby. My grandparents were not trying to have another child. Boy, when it happened, they were surprised and pleased as well.

Since his brothers graduated from high school and moved away before my dad started first grade, my dad grew up as an only child for much of his life. He missed his brothers and begged my grandmother to have another baby, but as you might guess, that was not in her plans! So, what did my father do? When he was around the age of 14 or 15, he brought a boy named

Pete home, and announced at dinner that he wanted Pete to be his brother and live with them.

To be fair, Pete did not have parents to care for him. He was not in a good situation. Pete had been living on the street and was becoming a juvenile delinquent without a family to care for him. So, my dad did what seemed natural to him with the core values his parents had taught him.

He brought Pete home for dinner and announced to my grandparents that Pete was going to be his brother and become part of the family. My grandparents were amazing people and after talking it over, they decided that taking Pete into their home was an acceptable and proper response to the situation.

Pete and my father made a pact to be brothers. After graduating from high school, they signed up and served in the U.S. Navy on destroyers. After their service in the navy, they both went to the same university and graduated from Pharmacy School together. They eventually got married and lived in opposite sides of a duplex so they could be together. Fortunately, their wives became best friends, so it worked out well.

As they started their careers, both took jobs in the same state to be close to my grandparents. However, it was my Uncle Pete who took a job back in their hometown. He remained there for the rest of his adult life, always taking care of my grandparents, and enjoying being close to his "adopted family".

As a young boy, I just saw Uncle Pete as my dad's brother, and we were all very close. It was not until I was older that I realized Uncle Pete had a different last name. Since it didn't matter to my dad, and he was my father's "brother," it didn't matter to us either.

I have learned that we create our own family just as we create our own life. If you want a good life, you need a strong set of core values. It is vital to identify your core values and to put them into practice. We must live by our core values. You see, we create our own family in life.

If you want your employees to share the same values, you must put them in writing. I suggest you place the list of company values where everyone will view them daily. In addition, it is a vital practice to discuss the core values regularly and for everyone to strive to live by them in the workplace.

We must live by our core values.

Mission Statement

A good mission has four key characteristics:
1) It is short and memorable, (10-15 words)
2) It describes who you are,
3) It explains what you do,
4) It defines who you do it for.

If every employee in your company cannot state the mission from memory, it is probably too long. Many owners that I meet cannot tell me their mission statement. They often say something like, "I wrote it out and have it somewhere". This type of mission statement is **useless**.

Unless, your employees can state the mission of your business, then your business will probably not achieve its mission very effectively.

Example:
ABC Company creates happy customers with quality service, kindness, & honesty for the _____ community.

One of the most important elements of a solid mission is that it contains "emotional" words that your employees and customers can relate to. Also, a good mission clearly identifies how the customer benefits. If these two elements are in your mission statement and your people can quote it from memory, then you are more likely to see your mission become reality.

Write a mission that contains emotion.
Additionally, your employees must agree with and believe in the mission. When a person goes to work with an internal agreement and commitment to your business mission, the employee will naturally be more fulfilled and more focused. Isn't this what you want?

Vision Statement

The vision statement is mostly for internal use. It also contains some important elements:
1) It has a clear timeline, (usually a date 3-5 years in the future)
2) It contains measurable results,
3) It will make your business stronger, healthier, and more sustainable.

All managers and team leaders must know the vision and talk about it regularly. The vision should play a key role in guiding management decisions, marketing, hiring, firing, and compensation strategies. Achieving the vision should be tied directly to compensation and future pay raises.

Your vision guides what you measure.

People need goals and targets. Your vision must be clear enough to achieve. The vision must be believable. In other words, your employees must believe they can and will achieve the vision. This provides both energy and direction to employees which builds their own self-esteem and sense of achievement.

Your compensation strategy is likely a strong contributor to your team's internal motivation, although they may not tell you this is true. While you cannot personally supervise every employee all the time, your compensation strategy will almost always guide their behavior.

We will discuss this in more detail in chapter five. What you measure gets attention. What you measure and reward gets done!

What you reward gets done!

Energy

Effective leadership involves having the energy to bring about change. There are many different leadership styles, but effective leaders all have one thing in common…the desire to bring about some kind of change and the energy and vision to execute their plan.

Having a motivating mission statement and a clear vision of where your business is going is one of the smartest things you can do. This gives your people something to connect to and commit to achieve. This taps into everyone's internal motivation and brings people energy.

When people are energized, you will spend less time trying to motivate them or get them focused. Instead, you will spend more time providing training, guidance, and helping them understand the "WHY" behind your "WHAT" and "HOW" in the business.

Working with positive energy is more important than putting in the time. Anybody can milk the clock to put in their hours. An effective worker doesn't think about "getting their 8 hours." Instead, their focus is on achieving the tasks that need to be completed on this day and by the end of this week. The effective employee is focused on achieving goals, doing things right, and completing tasks in a timely manner.

Effective leaders focus on results, not hours worked.

When you reward energy and results, you will attract the kind of team members that you need. You will also "weed out" people who do not model commitment and who are unwilling to change. You see, an effective business rewards people who are committed to do their job well.

If someone is not committed to complete the work they are hired to do, in the way you have trained them to do it, why would you want to keep them or pay them? It is simply folly to retain this kind of employee and expect that you can reach your business goals.

Motivation

What kind of motivation do you use in your business? There are two primary types – internal and external motivation.

Internal motivation taps into the core desires and needs of a person. When internal motivation is engaged, a person tends to be more focused and more energized. They consistently give more effort and energy to their work. This does not mean they do not make any mistakes, but their mistakes are not the result of not caring or not trying. In most cases, mistakes are just mistakes. Mistakes just happen.

External motivation is usually either a reward or the threat of some type of consequence. This kind of motivation is easy to use, but it has been so overused that it has lost much of its effectiveness over time.

External motivation requires managers to review results, to implement consequences and remember to provide the rewards that were promised. If a consequence is not consistent and the rewards are not forthcoming, then external motivation breaks down.

Internal motivation includes things such as:
- Personal pride in doing a good job
- Positive work culture
- Having a friendly environment
- Encouraging laughter in the workplace
- Sharing employee successes each week
- Focusing on things done right and outstanding results
- Communication about "who" we are and what "we do"

External motivation includes things such as:
- Spiffs for making an extra sale
- Bonuses for hitting company goals
- Rules in an employee handbook

- Fines or reductions in commissions for not meeting a standard
- Writing up employees for errors
- Threats of termination or suspension from work

Now, do not be confused. There is a place for external motivation. However, if this is mostly what we focus on, we are only addressing half (50%) of the motivation needs in our business. Last time I checked, 50% was still a failure.

Performance

So, you want to see high performance from your team? Welcome to the club...so does just about everyone else. The question is how do we achieve good performance consistently?

First, you must begin with your workplace culture. This includes your mission, your vision, your core values, and your approach to motivation. Remember that external motivation requires you or someone to review or observe behavior and decide how to reward it. Internal motivation provides its own reward. I encourage you to implement internal motivation as much as you can.

Second, people need regular feedback on their work. In order for anyone to improve and then sustain a desired level of quality, they need feedback on their work results. People also need a clear goal, so they know whether their actions are working effectively or not. Without a clear target and consistent feedback, it is futile to expect improved performance or dependable results.

This reinforces the idea that a manager must be a leader if his or her team is going to be a top-producing unit.

People need feedback and the #1 source they look to is their supervisor.

Good managers recognize, respect, & reward good work.

Train your supervisors to lead, motivate, and energize employees. We often ignore the need to train our managers, and they need ongoing training just as much as the rest of your team.

Results

Let me go ahead and put this out there…your business results are more of a reflection of your leadership than a reflection of your employees' abilities. Repeatedly, I find that employees are underperforming from 25% to 50% depending on how they are treated by management, how well the systems are working, and by how much they enjoy working in your company.

Research shows that one of the most important predictors of whether a new employee will stay or not depends on whether the employee is able to make a friend at work within 6 months or less. People are more likely to remain if they feel they fit and they are comfortable working with others.

Haven't you spent a lot of money to locate, identify, interview, and train new workers? How much energy and time do you spend making sure they "fit in" and find a friend in the workplace?

Research also shows that one of the most powerful predictors of worker commitment is how their manager makes them feel. If the manager is usually even tempered and approaches an employee with the desire to help them succeed, this is highly predictive of positive worker results. However, if the manager dishes out threats and/or is inconsistent in mood or temperament, then employee commitment and worker performance will both suffer greatly.

Positive results and high performance on the part of your employees reflects how employees view the leadership in your business. When employees feel valued and important, they inherently feel the need to do what is good and right for the company.

However, when employees are not doing what is right for the company it usually means one of two things:
1) The employee may not feel valued.
2) The employee does not respect others and may not respect themself.

In either case, no financial reward that is going to change the employee's behavior and commitment. High performers have a strong internal commitment to results.

When you recognize your best performers regularly and build systems to reward good performance, then most employees will adjust their performance to obtain better rewards and to be recognized for their performance.

__Reward employees who perform well and replace employees who underperform.__

Takeaways from this chapter.

- *Focus on wins and attract more positive results.*

- *Our thoughts and energy are contagious.*

- *We all have flaws and weaknesses.*

- *Good managers bring positive energy into the workplace.*

- *Culture is created daily.*

- *Employees respond to the attitude & energy of their supervisor.*

- *People who are your opposite are not your enemy.*

- *The purpose of life is to build positive relationships.*

- *Love is an action, not a feeling.*

- *Smart people create the life they want.*

- *What you reward gets done!*

- *Effective leaders focus on results, not hours worked.*

- *Reward employees who perform well and replace employees who underperform.*

Chapter 3
STAFFING

As the quality of your staff goes, so goes the quality of your company. Smart business leaders follow this principle: *"When you find a quality person, hire them."*

You will almost always have some position that a highly qualified, motivated individual can fill. A person with high integrity and a strong work ethic will more than pay for themselves. Owners sometimes fall into a negative pattern of thinking there are no quality people to hire. More often, I find quality people who have no idea that service companies are even looking for someone like themselves.

The service industry is often "hidden" from regular job seekers. When there is an opening, you place an ad to fill the position and as soon as you hire someone, you close the ad. Growing companies keep job ads open all the time.

It is always a good idea to have more resumes than you need. You want to have more people who want to work for your company than you can hire at any given moment. Now let's talk about why you probably need more technicians than you currently have on staff.

Technicians

Most likely, you have several levels of technicians with an assortment of skills. The most valuable and rarest of technicians is the one who has a high level of technical skills for diagnosing and repairing problems. At the same time, they are also skilled at suggesting, presenting, and selling new equipment when it makes good sense for a customer to replace rather than repair their home equipment. These techs typically have a strong commitment to the process, to quality, and have learned some good communication skills. Customers trust them and respond to their suggestions.

The next level of technician is skilled at diagnosing and repairing problems, and they also can set leads for upgrading or replacing equipment when it is a better choice for the customer. These technicians usually work in cooperation with a salesperson or comfort advisor to sell or replace equipment. These techs may have strong skills for diagnosing and repairing equipment, but they may lack the level of communication skills that are necessary for equipment replacement. However, all professional-minded people must be in a continuous training program for ongoing improvement.

The third level of technician is sometimes called a maintenance technician. They provide the annual or semi-annual home inspections and equipment cleanings or "tune-ups". These technicians can also be utilized for residential installations, light commercial remodels or installations, or as helpers or apprentices. They must have a strong work ethic, some basic knowledge of tools, and possess mechanical abilities.

Over time, they will develop more knowledge and improve their ability to diagnose and repair problems. Technicians must be taught how to present options and how to suggest add-ons and upgrades to customers. Since they have fewer technical skills, they should learn to rely on their "customer service" skills to generate revenue and bring value to your business.

When looking for technicians, it is more important to hire people who have good energy, are honest, have a good work ethic, and who are comfortable talking with other people. The best "repair person" is of little value, if they cannot help a customer become comfortable with their repair options and make a good buying decision. A great technician has a combination of practical skills and human communication skills.

You can teach a person with communication skills and a good attitude, how to do the technical part of the job. However, it is a supreme challenge to train a person with strong technical skills to be a good communicator and/or to have a positive attitude if they have no desire to engage in this area of personal growth.

Technicians must communicate to build trust.

All employees must learn and practice the following principle…the customer's #1 problem is developing trust in your company and feeling comfortable with your employees. When we win at this level, completing the repair or making a new sale is the easy stuff.

Installers

Your install team must consist of people with a high commitment to quality. They must be comfortable doing the same process on a daily basis with a high level of consistency. They must be willing to adhere to a quality checklist and to consistently complete their jobs to such a degree that nobody is required to follow behind them to touch, tweak, or adjust the equipment once they leave the home.

Installers must be committed to clean up after themselves and keep customers informed and satisfied. Although they do not spend as much time in communication with customers as a service tech or a salesperson, your installers should be able to ask the customer about any important additions or upgrades as they are installing their new equipment. It is vital to provide the highest quality comfort during the installation, rather than have your service techs come back and try to sell add-ons later.

Finally, a quality install includes time with the customer to explain how the equipment operates. Demonstrate the controls and help the customer get comfortable with their new purchase.

The Office Staff

The office staff typically consists of at least three key roles... CSR, Dispatcher, and Bookkeeper. These are three very different roles, and they require different skills and personality styles for the highest level of success.

The CSR Role

A CSR's job is NOT to take incoming calls. Their job is to fill the "Service Call" board for the week. This means they must have a plan to add maintenance calls to the board for the following week and starting on Friday afternoon and throughout the weekend, they must fill the Service Board with enough calls to keep your techs working. They need weekly goals.

Let's say that you have three technicians who average at least 3-4 calls per day. This means that you need approximately 45 to 60 service calls on your board each week. These may consist of a combination of maintenance and service calls.

You also need a financial goal for the CSRs and technicians. Scheduling a lot of calls each week without a clear weekly financial revenue goal is a good way to go broke or worse, pay your staff and not have any money left over to pay yourself.

So, let's imagine that you need each technician to bring in $1200 per day. That would equal $3600 daily (3 techs) and $10,800 weekly. Who is keeping up with your revenues to make sure you receive $10,800 each week?

Are the techs keeping up with this? Not likely, especially if they are paid on an hourly basis. More likely, your technicians are counting their own hours to be sure they make enough money to pay their own bills for the week.

What about your bookkeeper? By the time the bookkeeper knows what your weekly revenues were, you are already well into the next week, so it is too late for them to impact or increase revenues for the week that you fell short.

However, your CSRs and Dispatchers are the perfect staff to add up your daily invoices and track your financial progress. They also know which techs are more likely to do a thorough job and who is best at replacing or repairing the oldest equipment.

If you missed your $10,800 goal one week, do you think you would miss it by at least $100? If you are honest with yourself, when you miss your weekly goal, it is more likely that you miss it by several hundred dollars, and sometimes by several thousand dollars.

So, why not give your CSR and Dispatcher a reason to track your weekly revenue? What if you offered $50 every Friday for each CSR who books their number of weekly calls on the board and to each Dispatcher who makes sure the "right assignment" is made for each service call so the "right fit" occurs between technicians and service opportunity?

When the CSR and Dispatcher schedule the guys in a way that exceeds the weekly goal, reward them with an another $50 for every additional $2500 in revenues over your weekly revenue goal. You will be surprised how often your guys start achieving and surpassing your weekly and monthly financial goals.

The Dispatcher Role

Your dispatcher can make you a lot of money, OR they can cost you a small fortune in missed opportunities. Just as in the example with the CSR above, what do you think it costs you when your dispatcher sends an underqualified technician to service a unit that is 12 to 15 years old? Will this junior technician diagnose and service the system as well as a more seasoned technician? Will any add-ons be sold? Will a lead be set for new equipment? Or worse, will upgrading equipment even be mentioned?

You see, the dispatcher serves like the quarterback of your team. You can have great talent among your technicians, but if the dispatcher merely sends the "closest guys" or the tech who will be most agreeable, you are likely to have a business that functions on small profit margins and fails to meet your monthly breakeven costs.

Your business calls should be managed like a professional sports team. Before each game, the offensive coordinator has prepared a well-scripted playbook. During the first part of the game, the team runs the plays just as planned.

However, a smart coach has the flexibility to change the plays or players when the situation demands, or they see that the momentum has shifted. Does your dispatcher work with your service manager in such a way, that the best "plays" are called each day? Is the best technician sent on the right call at least 90-95% of the time? If not, you need to spend some time working with your quarterback (dispatcher) and your offensive coach (service manager).

Does your dispatcher know the score each week? By this I mean, do they know the weekly revenue goal, the monthly goal, and how close you are to meeting and exceeding the goal. You might be surprised just how diligently your dispatcher and CSRs can work to meet your business goals IF they know what the goals are.

In some businesses, if they are not close to hitting the monthly goal by the end of week 3, you can bet the technicians and the rest of the team are going to sit back and coast through week 4 of the month. Their mindset becomes, "what's the use, we are not going to make the goal." They know their manager or owner will be upset, but since they are paid hourly, they figure it's not their fault they didn't get better calls this month.

However, just the opposite happens in the best service companies. When they are still behind at the end of week 3, you can bet there will be a team huddle. The owner and managers will put forth some type of challenge to the team and "up the ante" by creating a sales special deal or giving an extra 1% or 2% commission for the last week of the month for those who hit a particular goal.

Some owners take pride that their team never works for a commission or is challenged to hit a "quota." This is

47

just plain foolish. Humans are created to achieve. We have amazing creativity and potential to accomplish a myriad of tasks. One of our greatest needs is to have a goal. This way we have something to measure our behavior and results against.

People hunger to have a challenge to achieve.

People have a deep need to feel they are accomplishing something. When you provide a realistic goal and your people achieve it, this provides a sense of satisfaction deep in the souls of your employees. Even money cannot provide the emotional peace and fulfillment that we get when we know we have done a good job and achieved what was expected or exceeded the goal.

When someone "tries to do their best" the truth is they almost never do their best. However, when we measure "our best" and then try again, we find that often, we can do "better than our best".

It is human nature to try to beat our best efforts. It is motivating to know that we achieved at a high level. It also means that our business is more profitable, and we will have the opportunity to provide performance bonuses to employees who put forth their "best effort" and worked to ensure the goals were achieved.

Once I told an owner that he should challenge his team to achieve a $1million dollar month in sales, service, and maintenance. When I asked him what his biggest month had been to date, he told me the previous year they had one month over $600,000. I suggested that if he set a big goal for his team to achieve, instead of a $600k month, that his team would have some momentum and energy, and they could meet a bigger challenge. In addition, a big challenge would help them stay focused and by achieving a bigger goal, they would earn bigger bonuses and commissions.

I saw this owner a couple months later and asked how the big challenge worked out. He told me that his team got so excited about the challenge, they had their best month over and surpassed $1.2 million in revenues more than double his best month to date. It was a major breakthrough for his team!

A year later, the same owner told me that his team came back to him and asked if they were going to do the same challenge again. He agreed and suggested they repeat the $1 million challenge. His team immediately met this suggestion with resistance.

The team felt the $1 million challenge was too small. They had already achieved that. They decided to do a $1.5 million challenge and guess what? They surpassed the goal again the next year and revenues for the month were over $1.6 million. He told me his team was ecstatic and they had a big team celebration picnic with Bar B Que and invited all of the team's spouses and children to celebrate with them. He wanted everyone to celebrate the achievement together.

You see having goals gives people a chance to win! And goodness knows, we need more wins these days. There is too much negative news in the media, and we are inundated with stories of poor customer service experiences. Give your team members something realistic to achieve and then be generous with pats on the back for their good work.

Give your team something to win.

Believe it or not, it is your best workers who worry about getting fired or losing their job. Your poorest workers do not worry about such matters. This is part of the reason they are poor workers. They just don't care as much.

However, if you give your good workers goals so they can prove their ability and value, they can sleep better at night knowing you would not get rid of your most "successful" team members. Goals help everyone know just how successful they really are.

The Bookkeeper Role

Every successful business has a solid, reliable, and timely bookkeeper. You need to know that the bookkeeper is a historian. They tell you what has happened in the past. They record and assign revenues, sales, and payments that have taken place in the past. So, I ask you, would you seek out a history professor or a history teacher for business advice? Probably not.

Bookkeepers and accountants are trained as "risk avoiders". They are taught to play it safe and to protect your business by following generally accepted accounting principles (GAAP). This is a good thing. Don't get me wrong. However, you are not likely to be very successful as a driver if you take all your trips by looking in the rearview mirror and driving in reverse.

Healthy businesses are guided by "forward-looking" owners. You need good data to know how solid your foundation is currently. You can spot trends in the sales cycle and economic patterns that help inform you in managing your business strategy. Keep in mind, that the future is largely created. Your ability to see what can be achieved and to build a bridge or path to success is one of your strongest skills.

You need the Profit & Loss statement in your hands within 7-10 days after a month ends. You must be able to view the previous month as compared to last year with both revenue amounts ($) and percentage of revenues (%) for each category. I also recommend a 6-month comparison to spot growth trends or declines.

Your bookkeeper must do job costing on your larger sales and they also keep an eye on the COGS % and Operations %. When there are fluctuations in expenses of any kind, a good bookkeeper is aware well before anyone else and they quickly inform the owner. When there are positive or negative fluctuations in revenues, a good bookkeeper informs the owner and suggests alternate strategies to protect profits and to achieve maximum benefit from gains.

In most cases, your bookkeeper can be part-time and work one or two days a week in the office. Until a business is doing more than $4 million a year in revenues, it is usually not necessary to have a full-time bookkeeper. You still need a CPA to review your books quarterly and to inform and advise you regarding your quarterly taxes, cash flow, and business equity. Do not assume that your bookkeeper has the knowledge of a CPA. This could be a big mistake.

Takeaways from this chapter.

- **Technicians must communicate to build trust.**
- *People hunger to have a challenge to achieve.*
- *Give your team something to win.*
- **How are your employees winning?**

Chapter 4
HIRING

As I stated at the beginning of the last chapter, *"As the quality of your staff goes, so goes the quality of your company."*

I cannot overemphasize the importance of having a strong, effective hiring process. When you train your employees how to interact with customers and how to complete a business transaction, you typically teach them a process to follow. Why do you do this? It's simple. A process that is repeatable and measurable, delivers more consistent results.

In hiring, you need a consistent process. It must be repeatable. It must be consistent. It must be ongoing. For your hiring process to deliver consistent results, you must be committed to using a hiring system.

Step 1
Recruiting

Most companies engage in recruiting when an employee leaves the business. This approach indicates that the business owner does not have a growth mindset. Why would you wait until you have a gap in your team to promote your business as an employment opportunity?

What are the odds that an outstanding, skilled worker is going to be looking for a new opportunity at **the same time** that you are hiring? Highly doubtful, isn't it?

Once I had this exact experience as an employee. I was in school in the mornings and had a job where my shift began at noon. My job was to climb into the attic of a new apartment complex and spray insulation 8-10 inches deep across the entire building. It was a hot, dirty, and itchy job. The insulation would fill the air so that you could barely breathe, and it would stick to your clothes so that no amount of washing could ever remove the "itchiness". I ended up wearing the same clothes to work every day because it was useless trying to get out the insulation through washing them. I hated this job.

Finally, one day it rained. Since it was raining, the guys outside the building could not load the insulation into the blower because it would get wet and clog up the machine. The field supervisor called off work for the day, so I decided this was the perfect opportunity to go job hunting. I didn't mind working construction, but blowing insulation was about the worst job I had ever done. I was determined to find something better.

Since I had worked in a bank for a couple of years as a part-time job in college, I decided this would be a good place to start looking. I put on my nicest shirt and slacks and drove to downtown Fort Worth, TX looking for the biggest bank. I figured the bigger the bank, the more employees they would have, so the better my chances they would have a job opening. Little did I know what was in store for me.

I parked and walked into the bank to survey the situation. Just looking over someone or some situation can often tell you a lot. Never underestimate the power of observation.

I observed a long counter of bank tellers who were handling transactions with customers. As I remember, there were 8 or more bank tellers. I walked up to the first available bank teller and asked her a simple question. Who is the lead bank teller? I know that every group almost always has a leader, whether it is an informal or actual role.

She told me that the last teller in the line to her left was the "head teller". I politely thanked her and walked down and got in the line waiting to see the lead teller. When it was my turn, she asked how she could help me. I told her that I had experience as a bank teller and that I was looking for a job in Fort Worth. I asked her how to apply for a position.

The head teller informed me that I would have to complete an application in the Human Resources office on the 3rd floor and she directed me toward the elevators. I thanked her and headed directly for the Human Resources office. Now it seemed that things were looking up for me.

When I arrived at HR, I made a new observation. This office was not staffed with "people friendly" personnel. The lady at the front desk motioned for me to sit in a chair while she continued a phone conversation. When she finished the call, she asked how she could help me. I responded that I was there to apply for a job as a bank teller. She told me that I would have to complete an application before anyone could talk with me. I requested an application and sat back down to complete it.

The lady in the HR office told me that I could take the application home to complete it and bring it back another day. I thanked her for the advice and shared with her that I had taken the afternoon off from another job and that I would prefer to complete the application onsite and have an interview that same day if possible.

Then she dropped a bombshell on me. She told me the bank only did interviews on Thursdays. I told her that unfortunately, Thursday would not work for me. I was off work due to the rain for that Tuesday, so I needed to find a job that afternoon if possible.

I asked if her manager was working that afternoon and she replied in the affirmative but told me that her manager would not be available to interview anyone until Thursday. I asked if there were ever any exceptions, and she replied "No". I told her that I had been hired by the president of the former bank where I worked in college and that I had excellent skills as a bank teller.

I asked if they could possibly make an exception and interview me while I was available at their bank, because I would not be able to take the afternoon off on Thursday if it was good weather again. It seemed that my only chance as dictated by this woman was to hope it rained on a Thursday if I was going to get an interview.

Then the most unusual thing occurred. As I debated back and forth with the woman in HR, I noticed that someone walked by the open door. Suddenly, I heard the footsteps stop. Then I heard them coming back in our direction.

A gentleman appeared in the doorway, and he asked the lady the same question, I had asked. "If the HR manager was in the office right now, then why couldn't she interview me at this time? Why did they only interview on Thursdays? Was there a chance they were losing potential employees due to this process?"

The woman picked up her phone to call the HR manager and mentioned that I was in the office waiting for an interview and then mentioned that the gentleman in the doorway was asking if she could interview me right now, since I was already in the office. Suddenly the manager's door opened, and she invited me right in for an interview.

Yes, it turned out the gentleman was the bank president. He had heard the conversation and wondered to himself if their hiring process was helping the bank get the best people, or was it merely more convenient for the HR staff?

Maybe I just got lucky. Maybe fate favors the determined. Maybe common sense prevailed that day. Regardless, I got the job that same day, and I went directly to the construction office, and gave them my notice. They thanked me for my service, wrote me a check, and told me that I could go ahead and move on if that is what I wanted. I started work at the bank two days later! No more itchy clothes or days filled with breathing insulation and dust for hours in attic spaces that were over 100 degrees. Success was mine.

I worked at this bank for the next few years. However, they made a classic error in hiring – they had made the process difficult for even the best potential employees.

Growing companies are always hiring when the right person comes along.

You should always be hiring good people. As stated earlier, a talented person with a positive attitude will almost always pay for themselves with flying colors. They bring good energy into the workplace. They help bring out the best in others and/or contrast with the negative results in your worst employees. A lot of success comes from having plenty of positive energy in the workplace.

Today, recruiting should happen 24/7. Good workers are usually looking for new opportunities. Mediocre workers are only looking for a new job. There is a big difference.

Why wouldn't you want a positive, skilled worker to apply for your position at night or on a weekend when your business office was closed? You need your application to be available online. Can potential employees apply for a job from your website? If not, then why not? Are you possibly missing out on some very good potential employees?

Did you realize that good workers can always find a new position? Other companies will recognize their attitude, skills, and experience, and hire them right now. Then who are you stuck with? Your worst employees will remain with you. Nobody is looking to hire them.

Advantages of Web crawlers vs Recruiting Websites

A web crawler is a specialized kind of recruiting website (such as ziprecruiter.com) that scans the internet looking for applications or employees whose skills match your job description. Make sure that you keep ongoing positions posted continuously for your most important positions, or at least a general ad indicating that you are always looking for "good employees" in your industry.

You want your business name to appear when someone is looking for a job or a new opportunity in your industry. The best people will not be looking for a position when the economy is strong, or you are having your best month in sales, or you are desperate for more good employees.

The best employees start looking for a new opportunity when work is slow at their current employer, or they get a difficult manager. This causes them to start looking for better opportunities. Your best potential employees may apply for a job when you feel you least need them. Hire them anyway.

Once they prove their value to your business and your team, you will have the opportunity to challenge your worst employees to improve their performance or help them find a new place to work if they choose to not improve.

Hiring a great employee when things are slow will not cost you more money. This will make you a lot more money. In many cases, owners find they can replace up to two of their poorest performing employees for every great employee they hire. This will save you in labor costs, and we have not even talked about how their higher production and energy can help you achieve double digit new profits by exceeding your business breakeven on a regular basis.

A good employee makes more money for you.

Headhunters

Headhunters will expect to be paid a percentage of the first year's expected salary when they are engaged in a personnel search for your company. This fee is approximately 10% of the expected first year's pay for the position.

If this seems high, you may need to remember that you will lose 30% to 35% of the normal revenue for the position for up to a year, when a new employee is hired, trained, and performing up to or above the same standard as your former employee. Better to pay 10% now than to drag out the process and pay 30% or more.

A big advantage of using a headhunter or professional recruiter is they have specialized recruiting tools, resources, networks, and processes to help you find and hire the best possible candidates for your key roles. If the position is directly linked to generating large amounts of business revenue, then I would be more confident in using a recruiting professional. You will get your money back, and a lot more, when you add a winner to your team.

Quality recruiters offer a "money back" or "free search" guarantee if you hire a candidate they suggest, and it doesn't work out. This makes the 10% fee a little easier to accept as well.

Another advantage of using a professional recruiter is their ability to search across the nation for talent, not just your local region. Often it makes more sense to hire a person with great talent and pay to move them to your location, than to hire someone with only average talent that costs you less to hire.

You get what you pay for!

Your team of employees is another good source for recruiting new employees. There are a couple of things that are very important to mention here. 1) Make sure your employees know they will not be blamed or held responsible if someone they recommend is later terminated. 2) Provide a "hiring reward" to your employee who recommends a new employee, rather than giving a "hiring bonus" to a new employee.

If your current employee receives a reward for recruiting the new employee, they are more likely to help you fill your job openings. I suggest you offer 1/3 of the hiring reward when the new employee finishes their first month. Then pay the next 1/3 of the reward at the end of the new employee's second month. Pay the final 1/3 after the new employee completes 90 days.

This limits the need to pay the full hiring reward until you have a chance to see how well the new employee performs. Pay for performance, not potential.

**Step 2
Testing**

Too often managers use their valuable time interviewing a person who is not a good fit, or who lacks the experience to fill your open position. Stop this now!

Put a solid testing process in place for all new employees. What kinds of tests should you use?

I suggest that you consider using assessments that measure general skills and aptitude for the position such as office skills, mechanical skills, or sales skills. In addition, you need to measure the applicant's potential to fit your culture and work environment as well. One of the best tools for this is an assessment of motivation, behavior, and values.

NOTE: Do not make hiring decisions based solely on assessment results. This is only one part of your interviewing and hiring process.

I suggest that you conduct a phone interview (10 minutes) first. Then send the applicant the links to the assessments or invite them into the office to complete the assessments, whichever is most appropriate for your business. I DO NOT recommend that you invest your time in a face-to-face interview until you have the assessment results in hand. You need some evidence to consider that can guide your interview questioning process. You should also have an application and possibly a resume' in hand prior to your interview with the candidate.

You need a scoring guide for your phone call. It does not have to be complex. I recommend a rating scale of 1-5, with 5 being the best score for each category. You can listen for the person's level of interest, their communication skills, their attitude, their energy, whether they were on time, their ability to focus, their ability to "think on their feet", their knowledge of the industry and your business, etc. Score each category 1 to 5 for each candidate immediately after the call. If you wait to score them later, you will not be as accurate or objective.

Make sure you score EVERY candidate on the same categories. As much as possible, ask every candidate the same basic questions to be fair. You can add questions for clarification when needed on a phone interview, but everyone should be scored on the same list of basic items.

I have provided a source for scoring guides to use on phone interviews at the end of the chapter.

Be well prepared for all interviews!

Step 3
Interviewing

Assuming candidates have completed their application, finished the assessments, and scored well on the phone interview, now you can invite them for a face-to-face interview. Typically, I suggest you only invite the top 2-3 candidates for a face-to-face interview.

If you feel compelled to interview all candidates, then at least have someone else do the first interview. You will find that 50% or more of the applicants will not make it to a face-to-face interview with the general manager or owner. This saves you time, but more importantly, avoids wasting energy on non-productive actions.

As the owner, it is critical that as much as possible, your energy is focused on productive activities and improving performance. You should avoid firefighting as much as possible.

Your job is to guide the team in the field to score touchdowns and put as many points on the scoreboard as possible. For you, this is measured in dollars!

Nobody should be more focused on being productive than you! Make sure your interviews are reserved for high potential candidates.

Interview Process
1 – Application completed and received in your office
2 – Phone interview (if applicant shows potential)
3 – Assessment emailed and completed
4 – Face-to-face interview with a manager
5 – Face-to-face interview with the owner or general manager

The owner or general manager should ONLY interview candidates that have successfully passed two or three previous levels of review. Do not waste your time as an owner by interviewing every applicant. Create a process that works for your benefit.

You will need a set of questions for each level of the interview process. You should have a set of questions for the phone interview, a different set for the face-to-face interview, and a final set for the 3rd interview. All three interviews should be scored using a standard interview rating scoresheet.

WARNING: Do not ignore this advice. Do not believe that only you can successfully "read" people. Do not believe that you will lose candidates if they do not get to see the owner first. There is a reason that other companies are bigger than yours. They have better processes in place. Improve your recruiting and hiring process.

You improve your hiring results when you involve multiple minds in the process.

Rating the Interview

Why do you need a rating scoresheet for interviews and how do you utilize this tool? One of the most common problems with interviewing candidates is the tendency to forget much of the candidate's responses within 15 minutes after the interview. Studies show that most often the last candidate interviewed is the one who gets the job because the interviewer tends to forget the responses of the former candidates.

A rating guide helps to avoid this problem by providing 8-10 items to score for each candidate. It also provides the opportunity to note the candidate's strengths and weaknesses. Finally, the interviewer may add personal comments about the interview.

Immediately upon completing an interview, the rating scoresheet must be completed by the interviewer. Waiting even an hour can skew the results as our emotions and memory take over. If you have multiple interviews, then plan at least 5-10 minutes between them to complete the interview rating guide. We need to score our perceptions within 5 minutes of completing the interview.

All rating sheets need to be completed by the final decision maker BEFORE making a hiring decision on a candidate. When you see the same concerns from two or more interviewers, this is likely going to be a problem in the near future.

You make better hiring decisions using a scoresheet.

Likewise, when you get general consensus on a candidate's positive potential, this gives the owner a greater sense of confidence to make an offer of employment. Involving more people in the interview process will lead to better and more consistent hiring. Will you ever get it right 100% of the time? Nope...I doubt it. However, you will greatly increase your percentage of good hiring choices by involving more than one mind in the decision-making process.

It is best to limit the first couple of interviews to 8-10 solid questions. If you want to utilize more questions from the interview guide, then you may want to include an additional staff member in the interview process and assign additional questions for them to rate the candidates.

The owner or general manager's interview should be the last step in the process. He or she should have copies of the rating sheets for the phone interview, any other face-to-face interviews and the results of all assessments before the final interview. This will allow the owner or general manager to explore any potential problem areas or areas of concern in more detail.

Use a standard set of questions for each candidate.

Interview Hint: Listen more than you talk. Ask questions and then be quiet. Let the candidates sell themselves. When you are listening, you are learning about the candidate. When you are talking, you are learning nothing!

You do not want to "sell" the applicant on joining your business. Your goal is to decide whether to invite the applicant to join your team. A "needy" interviewer comes across as desperate.

A confident owner will invoke a strong desire for applicants to want to join your team. Do not be afraid to raise your standards and you will find that you attract a higher quality of employees. Do not be afraid of offering incentives for good performance and you will attract top performers.

Remember, it is not how much you pay that matters most in business. Provide fair pay and provide a path for high producers to earn 30-50% more via production pay.

It is how much you produce and ultimately how much you keep as a profit that matters! When employees feel a sense of personal pride and enjoy the work environment, they are much more likely to stay. Most people who leave a business have more in mind than just the pay when they leave.

It is not how much you pay that matters most in business.

You want to base your hiring decision on solid data that you gather from multiple sources. This will give you a more well-rounded view of each candidate and their potential fit for your business. When you make a decision to hire a new employee, you should make every attempt for them to start as soon as is reasonable.

Take note of how a candidate left their former employer.

However, if the candidate "drops" their current employee without giving proper notice, do not be surprised if they later do the same to you. Observing a person's behavior will provide useful insights for you in regard to what to expect from them in the future.

Step 4
Onboarding

Onboarding is the most overlooked and most underrated process in recruiting and hiring. A solid onboarding process is seldom ever a waste of time. A really good onboarding process usually takes from 3-5 days.

The onboarding process should achieve some key goals which help maximize the energy of new employees in several areas. These are just a few of the benefits of a solid onboarding process.

1) Help new employees get to know the current staff
2) Help the team get to know the new employee

3) Allow time to assemble the needed resources
4) Provide a chance to get a feel for the work culture
5) Foster understanding of core values and expectations

Onboarding aligns with the fact that energy is more important than time. Getting a new employee working in their new role very quickly may seem efficient. However, it is usually not as effective. Helping a new employee feel comfortable in the new work environment will tap into more of their energy and effort.

Effectiveness is doing what produces the greatest results. Efficiency is doing what produces the fastest results. Focusing on efficiency can actually lead to more employee turnover. By helping new employees to acclimate to your culture they will form bonds with your team, and you get better results. New employees will have more energy, more focus, and achieve better performance and results much sooner.

Aim for effectiveness over efficiency.

Takeaways from this chapter.

- *Growing companies are always hiring when the right person comes along.*

- *A good employee makes more money for you.*

- *You get what you pay for!*

- *Be well prepared for all interviews!*

- *You improve your hiring results when you involve multiple minds in the process.*

- *You make better hiring decisions using a scoresheet.*

- *Use a standard set of questions for each candidate for consistent hiring decisions.*

- *It is not how much you pay that matters most in business.*

- *Take note of how a candidate left their former employer.*

- *Aim for effectiveness over efficiency.*

Chapter 5
Firing

Terminating an employee is not fun. However, if you are going to build a winning team, it will be essential that you eliminate people who are not going to be team players and those who are unwilling to implement your processes. You cannot build a successful team with workers who are not committed or willing to comply with your normal business processes.

You cannot build a winning team with employees who will not follow your processes.

When employees are confronted with issues of poor performance, they will usually tell you what they think you want to hear. The problem with poor performance is usually not due to the employee's ability. Most often the problem is the employee's beliefs and attitude.

When an employee says they are going to improve, I am not moved by their words. I believe that behaviors tell you more about a person than what they say.

If someone is a team player and has "buy-in" to your company, then their behavior will align with your goals and training. If their behavior is regularly out of alignment, then you have a lone ranger on your hands. This person is not going to be of much use to you over the long term, and they are unlikely to be successful on their own either.

Behaviors tell you more about a person than their words.

One of the reasons that coaching is so effective in business is because good coaching addresses the ways a person thinks. Everyone has some "false beliefs" that work against their best success. Some of these beliefs were taught to us by our family, some come from our interpretation of life events, and some beliefs arise from our personal experiences.

Behavior is usually a reflection of a person's beliefs.

The way that we arrive at a false belief is not as critical as recognizing the ways this belief works against our success. Let me give you an example.

Gut Feelings

People often ask me how long they should wait to terminate someone, or how many chances they should give an employee who doesn't match up to their standards, core values, or their expectations. My typical response is to follow the three-strike rule, just like in baseball.

The first strike receives a verbal warning and correction. The second strike needs to be written up and signed by both the employee and the manager. This serves as notification that things are getting more serious and immediate change is warranted. The third strike should be the employee's last day to work for you. In my experience, giving people more than three chances will only hurt your company and other employees far more than it will help the wayward employee.

Sometimes, the problem may not be that the employee is blatantly disregarding the company processes. Perhaps the employee is just not a good fit for their position. How long should you wait to take action?

The day that you realize the employee is not a good fit is the day you need to take action. Determine if you have another position that fits the employee's skills if they are a strong worker with a good attitude. If not, then do the employee a favor and let them go so they can find a position where they are a good fit. There are very few things more demoralizing to a person than failing at your job day after day, especially when nobody does anything to change the situation.

Termination Avoidance Strategies

How do you pre-fire an employee? I was consulting with a company in Missouri and the owner asked me what he should do about Bill, who was the technician with the most knowledge and experience on his team. The problem was that Bill produced the lowest revenue of the team and no matter what type call he was sent on, Bill would return with invoices that were far below the company average sale.

To make matters worse, Bill was the second employee hired by the owner's father-in-law, who was still involved as a key shareholder in the business. Bill had become a friend of the family who attended family events and Bill was a hunting partner with the father-in-law.

My recommendation to the owner was that he needed to give Bill a two-week notice that Bill would terminate himself if results did not change immediately. Then I offered to coach Bill to success. I gave the owner my phone number and told him to have Bill call me at 5:00 p.m. on Friday after he delivered the news about the two-week termination warning.

My phone rang at 5:02 p.m. and I knew an angry Bill was likely on the other end of the call even before I answered. After a few minutes of "expressing" his displeasure with me for advising the owner to give him a two-week termination warning, I told Bill that I understood that he was upset and that I would probably feel the same way if I was in his shoes. Bill paused for a second, and I asked him if he would like for me to help him keep his job.

He responded, "yes, if it is possible" and that was all I needed. I asked Bill a series of questions about his belief in the company, his feelings about the owner's family, and his connection to the other employees. Then we talked about his reasons for giving away work for free to customers he didn't even know, or doing work for customers at prices below the company goals.

Bill realized that his belief was that their prices were too high. He felt that he was "cheating" customers by charging the company prices because people could go online and buy the product at a lower price. He realized that he was hurting the company by giving away his skills for free.

Bill was not considering the fact that parts still needed to be installed and that his years of training and technical knowledge have a high value. With residential service, people are not buying a "part". Customers are paying for a professional inspection, a thorough explanation of any issues with their system, and they want several options to consider.

Wrong behaviors reflect false beliefs.

We discussed how prices had increased across the nation and the fact that the company prices were actually slightly below the national average. We also discussed the training that he had received and the fact that he was not following the company's process for presenting inspection findings and options for every customer. Bill's goal was to be a "hero" to the customer by charging the lowest price possible.

Once Bill admitted to his behavior, his mindset changed immediately. He told me that he was going to start following the company process and that he realized how his behavior was hurting the company. He admitted that he was being disloyal to his employer. I asked Bill to think of ways to improve his process and to call me on Monday afternoon to let me know how the day turned out.

On Monday, I received a call from Bill a few minutes before 5:00. He was excited. Bill told me that he had completed 4 calls on Monday and his invoices totaled over $1,400. At the time, the daily goal for the company was $1,000 with an average of $250 per service call. Bill continued to improve and by the end of the week he averaged over $370 per call. This was more than $120 over the company standard!

Finally, Bill realized that his job was to do a professional inspection and to provide several options, NOT sell the customer a part at a cheap price. Bill did not need to sell anything. By providing an honest evaluation and a thorough set of options, Bill was surprised to find that customers happily chose better options. He found out that people will buy good choices if you present them properly.

Everyone did not choose the best option, but very few chose the cheapest (band-aid) option. The result was that Bill's performance soared and he was soon a top producer with great customer satisfaction scores.

Bill continued to improve, and his average service invoice increased throughout the rest of the year. He finished the year as the #1 technician in customer satisfaction and in revenue production. In fact, Bill was asked to mentor a younger technician named Jay who was struggling.

Within two weeks the average invoice for Jay was nearly as high as Bill's. Jay finished as the #2 technician in revenue production for the company that year. Both Bill and Jay were the top two technicians the following year as well!

If an employee cares, he or she will change their behavior.

Termination Tips

What are the steps to terminating someone effectively? Consider the timing for termination. Try to avoid terminating an employee just before a holiday if possible. However, it is not always possible. It is better to terminate an employee in the morning than at the end of the day. Why have them put in another day's work just to let them go? This will give your employee the rest of the day to work through their emotions and to think about their situation.

Call the employee to their manager's office and have at least one other person witness the termination. It is important to have a second person to witness the termination as it can minimize emotional outbursts. However, some people are so emotional that no effort is going to avoid an emotional outburst from them.

Keep the termination notice short. Normally, a termination notice should take less than 2 minutes. The longer you talk, the worse the situation will get. Once an employee is notified of their termination, the best thing is to let them move on immediately.

Thank the employee for their service and let them know that things are not working out. You can refer to the fact that several notices have been given for behavior or performance and repeat that things just have not worked out. Again, thank them for their service.

Be a record player if the employee wants to argue. Just repeat your termination decision and thank them for their time of service.

Keep the termination notice short – less than 2 minutes.

Termination Check List

Why would you want a checklist for termination? Terminations are emotional for everyone. Unless you are in a situation where you terminate people several times a month, it is unlikely that you will get very comfortable with terminations. However, terminations are sometimes necessary.

You need a clear process in place to guide your behavior and decisions during this emotional experience. The last thing you want to occur is for the employee to keep your company shirts and invoices, and continue to work as a representative of your company, or to start their own business by using your resources.

Replacement

Recruiting is not usually fun and exciting. However, it is one of the most critical components for building a winning team. Great sports teams dedicate a significant amount of time and resources to recruit the best possible players.

When you recruit a new technician, CSR, dispatcher, installer, or salesperson, do they ever come from one of your competitors? The answer is probably yes. If so, you need to remember they will bring both good ideas and bad ideas and practices from your competitor.

Hire for attitude first. Someone on your team should be able to train and teach a person how to do any job in your business. You probably will not be very successful if you are trying to teach a person with a bad attitude to consistently have a good attitude.

Attitudes are contagious. A good attitude brings positive energy and attracts more people with a good attitude. Employees with a good attitude also create more trust with your customers.

Your business is NOT repairing people's HVAC equipment. Your business is to serve people by repairing their HVAC equipment. Many technicians get into the industry thinking they are just going to work on equipment and not have to deal with customers much. They may see your customers as more of an interference or a hassle.

The truth is that a technician must first recognize who is paying for the repair. The customer must be their first priority over doing the repair. If a customer doesn't trust or like the technician, it is unlikely the customer will consider options for maintaining or improving their system's efficiency.

You are in the people business, not the repair business.

Takeaways from this chapter.

- *You cannot build a winning team with employees who will not follow your processes.*

- *Behaviors tell you more about a person than their words.*

- *Behavior is usually a reflection of a person's beliefs.*

- *Wrong behaviors reflect false beliefs.*

- *If an employee cares, he or she will change their behavior.*

- *Keep the termination notice short – less than 2 minutes.*

- *You are in the people business, not the repair business.*

Chapter 6
Compensation

What is the primary role of compensation? From the company's perspective, compensation is a cost of operations. The lower the cost of operations, the higher the chance of making a profit, right? Hold on… not so fast!

From the employee's perspective, compensation represents their value as an employee. Thus, an $18 per hour employee is not as valuable as a $28 per hour employee, right? Wait a minute…we may be getting this all wrong.

You see, it is not the compensation that really matters, and this is where both managers and employees get tripped up and end up crossways with one another. What really matters, is the overall production of an employee compared to their compensation. It is entirely possible that an $18 per hour employee is the most valuable employee on your team. On the other hand, your $28 per hour employee may be your MVP.

My point is that unless you are comparing production to their compensation, you really have nothing more than a gut feeling about who is producing the most money and who is "overvalued". Your gut feeling is often wrong when it comes to compensation.

Motivation & Incentives

I am not a big fan of the "performance pay" movement. I've had clients who utilized this approach and I have seen it work as long as the service call board is full. However, when the board gets too full, performance pay actually works against the company's interests. When the board is not full, performance pay works against the employee's ability to meet their financial needs.

So, what do I suggest? I believe the most effective compensation plan is a hybrid approach. This includes a base pay model for technicians, installers, and office staff with an incentive program that awards your best performers for their production.

Yes, there will be a gap between a new employee and someone who has put in years or decades with the company. However, my belief is that someone is not worth more just because they have worked for your business for a long time. They are worth more if they produce more, and if they mentor and model the way for new employees to achieve the right results as well. This is why I am such a strong believer in using scorecards in the workplace.

Performance in the Goal

If you cannot measure performance, then how do you know who your best performers are? The truth is that you don't know. Just working more hours or on weekends does not make someone a better performer. It just means they are costing you more money, especially if they get overtime pay.

Instead, why not take the time to work with a business coach and build performance scorecards for each department in your company? When people know what matters, it changes their behavior.

Have you heard about the Hawthorne effect? This term was coined as a result of some experiments with the workforce of the Western Electric Company in Chicago. They found that when they reduced the lighting in the factory it increased worker productivity. Then when the lighting was increased, the worker productivity increased again. When the lighting changes ceased, worker productivity dropped back to the previous levels.

After interviewing their workers, they found that employees believed the lighting changes were because they were being observed. We know that when workers are aware their productivity is being monitored, people will work harder.

If you want better performance, focus on performance.

Additionally, if they believe their manager has an interest in helping them succeed, then workers become even more motivated to perform at their best. So, it makes sense that when we post performance goals and recognize the top performers, we tend to see overall performance for the team improve and begin to achieve the goals that were set.

Spiffs are Dead

Why am I negative about spiffs? Let me put it this way. When most spiffs were introduced a couple of decades ago, you could actually buy something for $10. However, unless you dine at McDonalds, you are going to be hard-pressed to find many items or meals that can be purchased for $10 today.

Spiffs are usually too small to matter to most of us anymore. Even a $50 gift card tends to barely draw the turn of a head. Life has simply become more expensive.

Incentivize the Results You Want

If you want to get someone's mind and heart in the game of business, offer them incentives for achieving the results that you want. This is what I mean. Let's say for example that you want your average service call to be over $300. We both realize that every service call will not be over $300. However, if we incentivize our technicians for every service call that is over $350 or $400, then we can be pretty sure that more service calls will be over $300.

Why do we set the incentive goal higher? We need to make sure there is adequate room to pay the incentive, and we need to make sure we hedge a bit to ensure our average invoice is over the goal of $300.

Some will say, okay, so your guys are just going to make false claims or suggest items that customers do not want or need. I find this kind of claim to be preposterous.

On the average service call, I can easily find $400 to $500 or more in add-on sales just by checking out the entire home. By opening the indoor and outdoor system, it is easy to identify whether there are additional needs the customer would want to be aware of.
- Do they need additional cleaning for the coils, the blower wheel, or the duct system.
- Do they have surge protection on both indoor and outdoor units?
- Some municipalities now require whole house surge protection for new homes or remodels.
- Are their smoke detectors over 10 years old?
- Is the CO detector over 7 years old?
- Is the water heater over 10 years old?
- What is their home water pressure?
- Do they have rubber or vinyl supply lines?
- Do they have an indoor air cleaner such as an Air Scrubber, Reme Halo, or Phenomenal Aire?

- Do they have 5 inch or 1-inch filters?
- Do they need a case of filters to keep on hand?
- Does the system have a float switch in the event of a drain blockage?

…and I could go on, but you get the picture.

I cannot tell you how many calls I have been on where the technician did NOT have an inspection form and did not review any findings with the homeowner. They did one simple repair and left the house thinking they did the homeowner a favor!

In truth, this approach cheats both the homeowner and the company. The homeowner likely paid a dispatch fee which should include a system diagnosis. How can a technician claim they did a thorough diagnosis if they had no checklist for consistency and provided no written report to the homeowner?

Even better, what if the checklist had green, yellow, and red boxes to check so the homeowner could know which items were the most critical? Homeowners may need to space out some expenses and evaluate which suggestions could be taken care of over time.

It's time we made the service call more customer friendly and created less sales pressure. Most homeowners will make better buying decisions if they are provided with the facts of their system's needs in a friendly, conversational manner. No arm wrestling is necessary, and technicians do not need to resort to any kind of shady behavior to achieve a solid and sustainable average invoice. Techs must follow the process they were trained to use. They must care about thoroughly explaining the issues, and the potential consequences of doing nothing. We need to do things the right way for every customer.

Put Compensation in the Employee's Hands

So, let's say that you offer your technicians 5% of the invoice for every service call over $350, it would increase their pay for the call by $17.50 for a call that takes maybe 90 minutes. This is equal to an $11.65 per hour raise for every call where the technician presents their findings, and the homeowner spends more than $350.

This is how you put compensation into the employee's hands. One of my clients did this, and boy, were they amazed at the results. The average technician increased their pay by over $9,000 that year. The company total revenues increased over $1.5 million, and their net profit increased by almost $500,000 over the previous year's net profit. How do you think the owner and the technicians felt about these results?

It feels natural to reward someone in proportion to their production. You see, a farmer plants more acres and considers improved planting methods for a bigger harvest. In the same way, your employees who continue to strive for improvement should be allowed to create the level of compensation they can earn.

You may want to consider a hybrid pay calculator that allows you to create a production pay program for your team. You can customize each tech's compensation according to their hourly rate, a percentage pay for setting up leads, a percentage pay for installations, and even a percentage for making equipment sales.

Bookkeepers tell me this approach saves them 2 to 4 hours for every payroll. Why not save money and time AND have more motivated employees?

Motivated performers need to achieve their desired income.

Takeaways from this chapter.

- *If you want better performance, focus on performance.*

- *Spiffs are Dead*

- *Incentivize the Results You Want*

- *Put Compensation in the Employee's Hands*

- *Motivated performers need to achieve their desired income.*

KEY THOUGHTS

Building a great team takes time. Your team's behavior and attitude will be determined by YOU. They will behave in ways that you are willing to tolerate. They will act based on how they believe you perceive them and based on the way they see you act.

BE THE CHANGE YOU WANT SEE
- Ghandi

Chapter 7
Coaching

First, what is the value of enlisting a business coach? Well, let me ask you this, would you mow your grass faster if you knew that you also had to clean out the garage and take out the trash? Or would you be motivated to mow the grass faster if you had the opportunity to use some "free" tickets to attend a sports game with your favorite team?

Likely, the enticement of free tickets to see your favorite team play would be more motivating. A good coach knows how to motivate people, starting with the owner. If the coach doesn't change the thinking and behavior of the owner, then it is unlikely that much of anything will change in the organization.

Owners sometimes think they are hiring a coach or trainer to get their technicians and salespeople on the right path. The truth is this. We are all on the same team.

No one department is going to make this next year a record-breaking year. It is going to take the best efforts of everyone, starting with the owner and the entire office staff, to the field staff, the salespeople, and the installers. We ALL have to change for the business to achieve its true potential.

Owners who are open to grow and change, quickly find their coach to be their best source of challenge, change, and results. If nothing significant changes in business operations, then it is unlikely that any major changes will occur in the work culture or performance.

If there are no major changes in operations, there will be no major changes in your results.

Second, where do you find a business coach who is going to actually help you improve your overall business operations so that you make more money? Great coaches are rare, however, there are several good sources of good coaches in the HVAC industry. Here are a few tips.

Ask your potential coach how many clients they are currently working with. If the number if more than 12, this is probably not your guy. This "coach" is acting like a business owner or service manager with 12 to 15 technicians. Do you think they get much individual time or attention from their manager other than when there is a problem?

There are only so many people that we can truly coach effectively. Many coaches struggle to keep up with even 10 clients. Few can coach more than 12 clients effectively.

What about contractor's groups or weekly group calls? These are not a bad source of good ideas. However, you will learn there is little to no accountability. Nobody is going to help you identify your problem areas. Probably nobody will call you out if you are not making the necessary improvements or if you miss a few calls. Groups can be positive networking experiences, but don't be mistaken and believe they can achieve anything close to what a coach will help you achieve.

Behaviors Are 1st - Time Management is 2nd

I often hear owners and managers complain about how busy they are and how they struggle with time management. I have watched many owners and managers go through your workdays. I have to say that owners and managers in the residential service industry are just as busy as owners, managers, and clients in other industries…EVERYBODY in leadership is busy.

The United States is known for having one of the strongest work ethics and highest expectations for work of any country in the world. We also have one of the lowest amounts of vacation days and holidays. Make sure your managers take two or three breaks during the year so they can stay fresh and energized during your peak seasons. The same is especially true for the owner. However, my observation is that many owners are good at taking time for themselves as their business grows, but these same owners are not the best at encouraging their managers to take time to recharge. Sometimes the owner is so busy enjoying their new freedom, they forget to encourage their managers to take time to refresh as well.

With that said, is our problem really time management? I do not think so. Let me tell you about an effective service manager that I have worked with.

James was responsible for a team of 16 technicians and the company also had 7 install crews (2-man crews) he was responsible for overseeing.

James came in to work early every morning. In this regard, he was just like most other service managers. It was not uncommon for him to be at the shop by 6:30 or 7:00 am at the latest. However, James did something unusual. He left work every day at 4:00 pm. Once I heard his reasoning, I had tremendous respect for his leadership.

James kept to this pattern of leaving work at 4:00 pm whether in the summer, or spring, fall, or winter. Every day he left at 4:00 pm. It turns out, James has a membership at a golf club. The city where he lives and works has the kind of weather that allows for golf almost 12 months out of the year.

When I asked James about this behavior, he said that golf relaxed him and gave him a chance to think through the problems of the day and to put them behind him. When I asked how he handled late afternoon issues or problems, he informed me that he tagged two of his technicians to be Lead Techs.

The Lead Techs took any calls from other techs after 4:00 pm. If there was a problem the Lead Techs could not handle, then they escalated the calls to James. He told me this only happens one or two times per month.

There are benefits to both James and the company. By recharging his batteries, James brings his best energy and focus to his work every day. FYI – the company consistently has a net profit over 20% and their revenues have grown by over $1 million each year for 18 years straight.

Leaders must recharge their batteries.

Energy and Focus Matter More than Time on the Job

If I have a choice between a guy committing to work 8 hours or a guy committed to give me his best effort until we reach our results, I will take the second option every time. Who cares if he works 8 hours or 5 hours as long as he gets the results?

From my perspective, too many companies have become focused on people "putting in their hours". This sounds an awful lot like a criminal "doing their time." Do you want people who put in the hours, or people who get results?

It makes more sense to hire great people who get the work done, and then create a work culture that allows for some flexibility and time off when possible. Companies that focus on production over hours worked are definitely more profitable.

I work with a client that allows two of their technicians to work a schedule of 4 days on and 4 days off. They share one truck which runs 84 hours a week. The guys work 4 (12 hour) days, and they get off 4 days. They have done this for several years and they love it. You get more production from one truck and your technicians are more rested and ready to go when they return to work.
You have almost no overtime for these guys and one of them is working every weekend. In fact, these guys offer to come in whenever another tech is sick, or the call board gets full.

Yes, most of their guys work Monday through Friday, and they take turns as the backup on weekends for on-call. All-in-all their technicians make a lot of money without working themselves into the ground.

Personal Goals Create Inner Harmony

Since I mentioned interviews, let me also say this…I want to hear an applicant's personal goals before I get too far into an interview. You will not believe how many times I hear things like "I hope to win the lottery" or "I plan to become a professional poker player". Is this someone that you can build a solid business around? I say, "NO WAY"!

You will do your employees a huge favor by helping them set personal goals to improve their family life, to take awesome vacations, to buy a new home, etc. Personal goals give us internal energy and a sense of personal pride and accomplishment. Achieving our goals helps us develop greater self-confidence and inner harmony.

Now if we are going to talk inner harmony, this brings me back to the earlier conversation about core values and personal beliefs. Give me a person who is living in sync with their personal beliefs and faith, and I will show you a person you can count on to keep their word and do what they say they will do. Personal goals tell us a lot about someone. Even more, goals paint a picture of the future the person is going to strive to build and create.

Takeaways from this

- *If there are no major changes in operations, there will be no major changes in your results.*

- *Behaviors Are 1st - Time Management is 2nd*

- *Leaders must recharge their batteries.*

- *Energy and Focus Matter More than Time on the Job*

- *Personal Goals Create Inner Harmony*

IS YOUR BUSINESS HEALTHY?

1) If you did not show up at work for the next week, would your business produce the same average revenues as when you are at work every day?

2) When you are around your employees, do you hear a good bit of laughter and good-natured joking?

3) Is your annual net profit before taxes, higher than 10%?

4) Do employees that you consider to be above average or excellent make more money each year?

5) Is the owner paying himself or herself a reasonable salary each month from the business?

6) Does the business have "cash in the bank" to sustain payroll for 60-90 days or more in the event of a major crisis or slow work season?

7) Do your employees show up for work at least 5-10 minutes before the workday begins?

8) Do your managers agree that positive energy is practiced by most of your employees?

Settle in and get ready for a good read. You are going to learn more about the path to profits, wealth, and freedom.

Chapter 8
Training & Practice

No winning team skips training. In fact, research on medalists across 18 different Olympic sports showed that the winner of the gold medal was more focused during practice, and spent 10-12% longer each week than the second and third-place athletes. Professional athletes practice hard every day.
(Bruzda, Natalie. https://www.unlv.edu/news/release/gold-line-olympic-athletes-and-their-focus-attention).

So why do your employees not have a weekly training regimen? Are you satisfied with second-rate performance? In your work culture is it okay to do a mediocre job?

You see, it is human nature to preserve energy. Unless we have a specific goal and have a regular training process, we only deliver our best performances sporadically. Consistent high performers train and practice on a daily basis. They review and refine their process. They compare data to see what is working best. They set goals and achieve them.

Weekly training is both critical and easy to achieve. Set a day for training each week and stick to it. For instance, if you set Tuesday morning as your training time, then your team should expect to train at least 44 to 46 weeks of the year. You will miss occasionally if you are on vacation or during holidays, or on the busiest week of the year, but overall, your team should expect to train every week.

Topical Training

There are plenty of topics to train on. I suggest that you spend 3-4 weeks on any topic that you bring to your team. Some suggested topics are:
1) Greeting the customer – 4 things to do every time
2) Building rapport – 3 things you always want to ask about
3) Creating confidence – personal credibility, company credibility, pricing process
4) Diagnosing the problem – what are the 5 things you will be looking for
5) Inspecting the system – give them a copy of your inspection form, ask the customer to read your maintenance program, inform them you will make a list of anything you find and sit down to discuss their options
6) Reporting on findings – why you want to sit at the table, how to cover the red, yellow, and green items, how to write up options
7) Presenting options – starting with the most comprehensive down to the band-aid option, creating a hybrid option
8) Closing the call – get agreement on the best option, why does the customer like this option, present the value of the company, present the maintenance club, and explain why it is essentially "free"
9) Future considerations – asking for referrals, getting customer reviews, leaving company merch (bottle openers, jar openers, plastic cups and/or bottles, calendars, grocery lists, etc.)

Each topic will need several weeks of training for your team to put it into practice effectively. I also suggest 10-minute standing "huddles" each morning to remind your team of the weekly goals and to emphasize the training for that week. People improve faster with daily reminders. Below is a suggested pattern for training:

- Week 1 – Cover the topic and have the team take notes on it. Discuss what they learned and how they will apply the knowledge.
- Week 2 – Review the topic again and discuss how the guys implemented the learning during the week. Have each person give a positive example and if they have a bad or poor experience share that as well.
- Week 3 – Have 2 or 3 guys demonstrate how they are implementing the process.
- Week 4 – Have the guys report on their achievements for the month. What were their individual goals? What are the team goals? How can they finish strong?

Here are a few more suggestions for an effective training program:
1. Focus on 6-8 weeks of training on 2 or 3 areas that need improvement. Take a couple weeks off and then start again. When you start back up, you may want to take the first training session to review or have your team demonstrate their skills to one another. Avoid using the term "role play" as most people dislike role play. Instead call it "skills practice" and have the team demonstrate to each other so they can all learn from one another. This way they can provide feedback to each other.
2. Train for 2 weeks on a topic and then have "skills practice" for 2 weeks on the topic. Change to a new topic after you see the results improve on the team scoreboard.
3. Create a schedule of training topics for each quarter. You will likely want to include some "technical" training on equipment and computer software updates as well as service training.

Weekly training is much easier to sustain if you already have the topics planned.
4. Hire a professional trainer who can provide "live" training for 40-50 minutes each week. All that is required is a large screen television and a webcam with a built-in microphone. There is something powerful about bringing a new "voice" to your training.

Your trainer will likely say many of the same things that you have already told your team. However, your team will incorporate the training faster and put it into practice more effectively. A professional trainer is less threatening than the owner. A trainer is more likely to utilize proven training techniques that work. You will find that it is a small price to pay for significant returns on your investment.

Invest in training, so your team is always improving.

Technical Training

There will be 2 or 3 months during the year when you need to emphasize technical training. Prior to the fall season, you will need to spend time training on the maintenance process. Even technicians who have done maintenance for years will still benefit from practicing the process, and teaching newer technicians how to complete the process according to your company standards.

Another key area of technical training will also focus on getting ready for the repair season. There will be new models to review and even good technicians are not likely to be as thorough as their manager or owner. Never assume that your technicians spend as much time thinking about the process as you do. Train them and have them practice in front of you and the team. You need to see what they do; not just hope they follow the process the way you expect. People do what you expect IF you inspect.

In the spring, you will need to spend a few weeks on new equipment and upgrades. Even the best professional athletes go over the basics at the start of a new season. They have mental muscles and physical muscles they need to get in shape. Technicians are the same. They need to be reminded and retrained over and over.

Plan out your training on a monthly basis and plan it for the full year. Do not wait and try to think week by week what you want to discuss. If you have the 12 monthly topics, it will make each week so much easier to plan and to carry out.

Video Training

There are several quality video training programs that you may want to consider. IMPORTANT NOTE: The video is only ½ of the training. You must lead a discussion on the video training as the other ½ of the training. Unless the guys discuss what they watched, they will NOT likely change their behavior. You need to ask the guys to commit to change if you really expect them to start practicing the new behavior.

HINT: I have learned that if I ask the technicians to raise their hand to commit to a new practice, they are usually faithful to put it into practice. Good technicians are naturally guys who keep their word when they commit to something.

Practice Training

I have given up on "role play." Technicians and salespeople both seem to have a deep dislike for role play. Instead, I tell them we are going to practice what we are learning. If they can demonstrate the behaviors and processes inside the training room, they will find it is super easy to do this in front of the customer.

I remind them that their favorite professional sports teams practice 5 or 6 days every week. They do not call it "role play". However, they run through the steps for every play and process that was discussed in the training room. If your team is going to be "championship" performers, then practice is not an option.

Summary – Weekly "Take-aways"

Guys remember better if you finish your training session by asking everyone about their "take away" for the week's session. If a guy can tell you what he learned and what he plans to do with it, he is likely to be growing and improving.

Review the Data

Successful businesses have scorecards for each department. If you want your people to experience personal fulfillment, they need goals or targets to aim for. People never do their "best" without a goal. Even when they have a goal, people usually can do even more after they achieve their goal, and you might need to set stretch goals for your best employees.

Scorecards act like a speedometer for your business. They will let you know whether you are on track to make a profit, if you are going to hit your breakeven, and if your employees are on track to receive a monthly or quarterly bonus. You only need to have 4-5 items on each scorecard.

The typical scorecards you need are:
- a technician scorecard,
- a CSR/Dispatcher scorecard,
- an installer scorecard,
- a sales scorecard, and
- a business scorecard.

Annual Planning

Every time I coached a business that achieved double digit net profits, I found they accomplished this feat AFTER they built a solid annual business plan. It takes 1-2 days each November for the owner and managers to meet and review the previous year's good, bad, and ugly results. It is also helpful to have all of your employees complete a SWOT analysis of the strengths, weaknesses, opportunities, and threats.

Finally, you will want to review the number of service calls, number of maintenances, and number of sales for the previous year by month. Then you will want to plan the number of calls, maintenance, and sales that you intend to run the next year. You want a plan to increase your average invoice for all three areas, and then you can multiply your expected invoice totals times the number of projected calls to determine your potential revenue.

Plan to achieve the revenue that you need.

If you want to increase your invoices and revenues, then you will want to really dig into the chapter on compensation. You need for your employees to be self-motivated to reach the monthly business goals. If they have added "carrots" to go after, you may be surprised to find out how much more your employees can achieve.

Daily Huddles

The daily huddle is very important for two reasons.
#1 – It gets your team together at the start of the day. People work harder as part of a team. Nobody wants to be the slacker or to let down the team (if they are a good worker).

#2 – People need to be reminded about the daily goals and expected behaviors. Maybe they are tired today, or stressed about a family situation, or not focused for any reason. Having a huddle helps get everyone on the same page and is a proven method for improving performance results.

This is the perfect time to affirm employees who are doing something well, to correct any actions that were not up to standards, and to provide coaching advice so the rest of your team can succeed.

Performance Evaluations

Most companies have an annual evaluation. This is a very poor practice. Do you think that telling a person once a year what they can improve upon is adequate to get their best performance?

Coaches provide feedback to their team members every single day! They do not wait until the season is over. How ridiculous would that be? They review each game AFTER is it over and before the next week's game so they can perform better.

If your team is not getting better each week, then you need to improve as a coach.

Studies show that 90% of the time, the source of failure is not due to your people. Most of the time, the source of problems is due to your system and processes, lack of training, or poor coaching. If you want your team to perform at their highest level, then you must train them, coach them, and evaluate their performance.

Effective evaluations occur at least 4 times per year. Before you say that you don't have the time to do evaluations this often, let me challenge the way you do evaluations. Do you fill out the evaluation on your employees and then meet with them? Stop it!

Instead, have your employees complete their own evaluations and then present their evaluation results to you as their manager. Now you can review their evaluation and offer your insights and feedback more effectively.

If you want your employees to keep improving, you must have regular conversations about their successes, their growth areas, and suggest new practices and training to help them improve. When you are focused on improvement more than criticism, it is amazing how much better your employees will respond to the evaluation process. If you tie bonuses or incentives to employee improvement, you will experience greater commitment and focus on performance on the part of your employees.

- Training
- Tech Performance
- Installer Performance
- Sales Team Performance

- CSR Performance
- Dispatch Performance
- Bookkeeper Performance
- Business Performance

Training & Evaluation

How often do you evaluate your employees' performance? If your answer is not "weekly" then you are giving up a lot of MONEY by your oversight or lack of feedback. Employees need weekly feedback on their work and production. The more specific the feedback, the faster you will see change.

A scorecard is absolutely vital for business success.

Company Scorecard

There are several KPIs that are proven to have a positive impact the net profit of a business. Why would any business owner not want to know how your business is performing every single week? What KPIs do you think successful company owners focus on? I can guarantee their main KPIs are linked directly to business growth and profitability.

Technicians and Service Results

My guess is that most of your technicians may be men. Guys, for the most part, have been conditioned to be competitive throughout their lives. However, once they join your business team, have you continued to challenge them to compete to achieve the right "behaviors" which drive your business results?

An effective technician scorecard measures results such as:

- The number of non-club member calls and the % who were signed up as club members
- The number of service calls run on equipment over 10 years or 12 years old
- How many replacement leads were set up
- How many customer reviews were requested and how many were received
- The average revenue created per hour per person
- The ratio of each person's revenue to their compensation (true value of a tech)
- The daily average per person … and more.

You get the idea. Now you are probably thinking, I don't have time to calculate all this information. No, you don't. I agree with you.

This is the reason you need a quality CRM software program that can print out the reports with the data you need. Then you simply take 20-30 minutes each week and update your technician scorecard.

Once you begin using a scorecard, you will find that it becomes the first thing your guys look at when they come into the office. They want to see where they rank. Everyone cannot be #1 in EVERY category, but every tech should strive to be #1 or #2 in **SOME** category.

Sales

What kinds of items do you want and need to track on your sales scorecard?
- Total proposals
- Total sales
- System sales vs. component sales
- Marketed leads
- Former customer leads

- Club member leads
- Technician set up leads

You will discover that some of your salespeople are better at marketed leads while others do better with tech leads. Make sure you are not "burning" leads by assigning them to the wrong person.

In addition, a well performing company will achieve an equipment sale for every 4-8 service calls as an average for the year. In some slow months, it may take 10 service calls to achieve an equipment replacement sale. In your busiest months, you should easily see a sale for every 4-5 service calls.

Some of you will read this and think it is rubbish. However, I have yet to find a single company that did not achieve these results once they focused on sales by using a scorecard.

You see, a man can go to the refrigerator or the pantry looking for something and then report with full confidence that it is not there. Now they think they need to go to the store and buy a new bottle of "such and such". However, a woman will see right where the bottle is in her mind and walk straight to the refrigerator or pantry and pull it right out.

Why is this? A man's brain is wired to think compartmentally. If a man is operating in the repair compartment of their brain, they often do not think about the age or poor efficiency of the equipment they are repairing. They just repair it and move on. This may end up costing your customers hundreds or even thousands of dollars in extra utility costs over a 2 year or 3-year period.

It takes more reminders to get a man to change his habits. When you are getting sick of reminding your guys about how many replacement sales you need for the month, they are just starting to think about setting leads for replacement sales. Don't stop reminding your team about this key component of your business operations.

Install Effectiveness and Efficiency

- How many "manhours" do you average per installation?
- How many "revenue dollars" do you average per install hour?
- How many callbacks do you average per 10 installs?
- How many installs take more than one day?
- How many Friday installs get finished by 4:00 or 4:30?

Why should an installer care about his effectiveness or efficiency if you cannot provide him with accurate and objective feedback to let him know how he compares to the industry average? Installers have bills to pay just like everyone else. If they are paid by the hour, they are going to work more hours to make more money.

Notice that I did not say they would accomplish more work. They will just "put in" more hours on the work clock. Why wouldn't you pay your install teams for production and good performance instead of encouraging them to work slower and put in more hours on each job?

When you create internal incentives for your installers to improve, you can create a quarterly bonus program that will keep your best installers with your company forever. The best part is it costs your business nothing, nada, $0.

Maintain a Full Call Board (incoming and outgoing calls)

- How many maintenance calls do you need pre-booked each week?
- How many slots do you need to keep open per technician for breakdown/demand calls this week? (It varies by season.)
- How much money do you need to bring in from the service department this month?
- What % of incoming calls are you booking?
- What % of outbound calls are you booking?
- How many club memberships are sold each week over the phone?
- What special offer do you have in place for your office staff to make outbound calls if the service board is not full?
- Why are you waiting for your phones to ring, when you have people fully capable of dialing the phone and making former customers or new customers' phones ring?

Takeaways from this chapter.

- *Invest in training, so your team is always improving.*

- *If your team is not getting better each week, then you need to improve as a coach.*

- *A scorecard is vital for business success.*

- *Energy and Focus Matter More than Time on the Job*

Chapter 9
Pricing

Pricing is one area that causes many owners to lose sleep at night. It is the source of much unnecessary fretting and worry. Why do so many owners worry about pricing? They are still thinking like a technician. Wow, that hurts a little huh?

So, let's explore a few questions. Hopefully, you will find some invaluable answers that will give you greater clarity and more confidence to price your products and services properly.

How do you price? Owners often use the following logic when this question is raised –
- My market will not sustain higher pricing
- Our competition is priced lower than…
- Customers won't pay more than….

Your average service revenue MUST generate approximately 65% to 80% gross margin. A more expensive repair such as a coil replacement may have a slightly lower gross margin, but your lowest two or three levels of repairs should be at 75-80% gross margin.

Trust me when I say this, a customer is not going to know much difference, but your bottom line certainly will. Here are a couple examples:

Actual cost for a part and labor = $50
60% Gross Margin = Price of $125
70% Gross Margin = Price of $167

Do not raise prices by adding 10% to your old prices.

Increasing your gross margin by 10% will put an additional $52 into your gross profit which is equal to your actual costs. However, raising last year's prices by 10% will only put $12 into your net profit, which is likely the reason you are not making any money at the end of the year.

Why do you price the way that you price? When the truth comes out, most owners price out of fear. Rather than having full confidence in their pricing model and the value of their products and services, they default to what they "feel" their market will pay.

There is always a demand in the market for quality. Yes, some people will buy the cheapest item regardless. Have you ever noticed that Ford truck owners usually continue to buy Ford trucks? The same is true for Chevy and Dodge. When a customer believes in the VALUE of a product or service, it is very difficult to sway them to change.

The problem in most service businesses is not the price. The problem is that your value is too low. You either do not promote your value often enough, or you do not provide enough value in the customer's eyes. Do you project a strong enough belief in your value? I have coached countless customers who increased their gross margin and grew by $500k up to $2million or more the following year.

All the while, the former owner (their father) was saying, "You are going to price yourself right out of business". Two years later their father was amazed at how wealthy his son had become and how profitably the business was operating.

Do not have low prices. Have high value.

What if there was a better way to price? Would you try it? ...Or would you make excuses that you "can't do that"?

Some of the most successful service businesses around, have their entire service prices on one page. Yes, that is right. They print several levels of prices and group together service items so that 90% of the most common service repairs are listed on one side of one page.

Keep it simple. You can make a lot more money by focusing on the average cost of repairs and grouping items together, than by trying to get the price "exactly" right on each call.

I can guarantee you one thing – you will get the price "exactly low" if you are doing pricing the old-fashioned way. If you want better results, then you need to decide to change your pricing model right now. If you keep pricing the same way, you will keep getting the subpar results that you have been getting.

Keep pricing simple.

How often should you raise prices? If I had my way, every service company would raise the prices for one or two levels of service each month. This would create a very small and very slow process for increasing prices that would cover all service items each year.

Many fast-food chains raise prices every month on a couple of items. This way, the customer doesn't notice. It may only be 15 cents, but at the end of the year, the prices overall will go up from 25% to 35% and business never slows.

However, many contractors do not have software in place that is sophisticated enough to raise prices this way. Therefore, I suggest that you raise all service items related to hot weather repairs at the end of each February and all service items related to winter repairs at the end of each August or September. You want to raise prices BEFORE a seasonal period, not after it is over.

You want to raise service prices for repairs just prior to the start of the next season of demand. This means it has likely been a year or more since any demand customers had their last service call. Most will not know if your price for their repair increased by $20 or by $50.

Raise service prices prior to each high demand season.

Equipment Pricing

Do your vendors increase your costs for equipment each year? I bet the answer to this question is a big "YES". Do they apologize – "NO".

If your costs increase, you have only two choices: 1) Raise your prices or 2) Lower your profit. So, I ask you, are you in business to make money or to provide your services like a non-profit?

Now, do not get me wrong. I strongly believe that your business should afford to offer one or two special "gifts" of new equipment each year. These should be strategic, and you should do this to either help one of your employees, or an elderly couple, or a veteran who truly does not have the financial means to keep their home safe and comfortable.

When you do these kinds of things, I believe you receive blessings back in many ways. Your employees will be proud of your company. The people you help will most likely tell others. You will eventually be known as the "good guys" in your community.

However, most of the families in your community have jobs and they work. If they cannot afford to replace their system, they can most likely afford to replace a major component each quarter or finance the costs. However, many, many homeowners think they are saving money by repairing their old system. More often the truth is that the customer is paying the utility company more than it would cost them to replace their system with brand new equipment, with a 10-year warranty, and with a low monthly payment plan.

When you bought your last truck or car, did you receive a 10-year bumper-to-bumper warranty? My bet is that it was more like a 3-year or 5-year warranty with a 72-month payment.

Service companies do not give themselves enough credit. You are replacing one of the most important items for a homeowner that works 24 hours a day, 365 days a year. It runs probably 10-20 times more than an automobile. It lasts 3-5 times longer than most automobiles. It comes with a warranty that lasts twice as long and it can be paid off in a shorter time frame.

On top of all that, the average homeowner will pay another $18,000 to $28,000 over the next 10 years in utility costs alone. By saving just $50 a month in utilities, the homeowner would save $6,000, plus have no repair costs over the next 10 years.

Do the math and I think you will agree that replacing equipment older than 10-12 years is probably one of the lowest costs a homeowner can experience.

One of my best friends told me that he paid for a repair over $800 on his HVAC system. When I asked him how old it was, he told me it was over 18 years old. He also shared that his average utility bills were over $600 per month in the summer in Texas, and his annual utility costs were over $4,500.

Educate homeowners and they will buy better solutions.

I encouraged him to call a friend of mine who owns an HVAC company. My friend ended up replacing his system over the within 4 months when it broke down again. His new payment was less than $150 for the new system (over 60 months) and his utility bills dropped over $400 the next month. Do you see how we are hurting our customers when we try to save them money with another low-priced repair? Customers need for us to educate them better.

A cheap repair may be the most expensive thing you do to a homeowner.

Equipment Markup

Your gross margin is often going to be a little flexible depending on your total costs for equipment installation. For instance, you may have a higher markup on a coil replacement or heat exchanger, which might cost approximately $1,000 to $1,500 in parts and materials. This job may have a markup of 60% of more, thus the price would be approximately $2500 with up to 4 hours of labor for a coil replacement.

However, a condenser and coil replacement would likely be at a gross of 45% to 50%. For example, let's say you sell a 3 ton, 2 stage system and your equipment and material costs are $2300. You would likely budget another $600-$700 for install labor (if you have your own installation crew) and another $350 for sales tax, permits, and contingency, bringing your total costs to around $2,950. So how much do you want to charge for this system?

At 45% gross margin, your selling price would be $5,296 with a gross profit of $2,384 (Gross profit is before you add overhead costs).

At 50% gross margin, your selling price would be $5,826 with a gross profit of $2,914. Do you see how the additional $530 price increase went to your gross profit? With a system replacement, your gross margin could range as high as 55% to 60% in the summer months.

For example, let's say you sell a larger system, or a tankless water heater and your equipment and material costs are $4,900. You would likely budget another $700 for install labor (if you have your own installation crew) and another $600 for sales tax, permits, and contingency, bringing your total costs to around $6,200. So how much do you want to charge for this system?

At 45% gross margin, your selling price would be $12,620 with a gross profit of $4,972 (Gross profit is before you add overhead costs).

At 50% gross margin, your selling price would be $13,837 with a gross profit of $6,100. Now you have an additional $1128 that drops right to your bottom line.

This is when some owners drop their gross margin to 40%, meaning the price drops to $11, 605 with a gross profit of $4,033. Some are convinced they need to sell their best equipment at a lower margin and their lower priced equipment at a higher margin. In this example, you would give up $2,067 in gross profits. Lowering your gross margin, means you would have to sell 30% more equipment just to make the same gross profit as you would have made at 50% gross margin.

How you choose to run your business and price your work is your business. However, you deserve to know what your choices are costing you.

Contact me to receive an easy-to-use tool - Gross Margin & Net Profit Pricing Tool. You can know your gross profit and net profit on EVERY sale BEFORE you close the deal.

Sales Commissions

Most commonly, sales commissions are paid at 6-8%. However, there are plenty of ways to pay salespeople as you can imagine. I have seen companies pay them by the hour with a 2 or 3% commission. I have seen companies pay them a base of $400 per week and up to

$1000 per week, with a lower percentage for sales. Some companies pay different commission amounts depending on the system level (Ex: Platinum level systems pay a higher commission than silver level systems).

The real question is this: *What is the best way to pay salespeople to maximize sales and profits?*

I am a firm believer that most people need more education about how a system works and the benefits of spending more money to purchase a higher efficiency HVAC system, or tankless water heater, or top of the line electric panel or generator.

Purchasing the highest quality system is usually a decision based on more than just energy cost savings. The customer who buys the highest efficiency system is often just as concerned about total home comfort, air quality, and other factors as well as energy savings.

So which level system requires more expertise, more education, and a higher quality sales presentation? When looking at things this way, I am an advocate for paying a higher commission for your highest level of equipment.

Likewise, which system takes the least amount of explanation and is typically a sale based solely on price? This would be your lowest level system or a furnace only sale or a coil and/or condenser, or a 40-gallon tank water heater, etc. I have no problem with a plan that offers a commission of 2-3% less for the lowest priced and equipment with the lowest energy savings rating.

Commissions that are calculated after the sale and based on the gross margin are both confusing and discouraging to your salespeople. Your sales team needs to know what kind of reward they can expect when they make a sale. This is likely their primary reward for success in their sales role.

You can add the sales commission to your calculated selling price and let the customer pay the sales commission. You still make the same gross margin regardless of the final sales price.

Let the customer pay the sales commission.

The rest of your team does not have to worry themselves over whether they will get paid at the end of the week. They are either on an hourly wage or a salary, so they know they will have a paycheck coming each week.

Have you thought about how your salespeople are feeling each Monday? They start every week with the prospect of no paycheck. They know their last certain paycheck was last week. This week, they can expect nothing unless they are successful in making some sales.

If you have never worked as a full-time, fully commission-paid salesperson, it is likely that you have no comprehension of the emotional strain that Monday can bring, especially during a slow month. When a salesperson takes a week of vacation, they are usually taking time off without pay…no sale equals no pay. Every Monday, they begin a new week with no expected income until they make another sale.

This is one reason that some companies have resorted to a base pay for the sales team. The challenge is that it lowers their reward for each sale by lowering the sales commissions. In addition, it can provide just enough security to lower the motivation to sell. Therefore, I do not advocate having a base pay rate for your sales team.

The best salespeople have several ways they manage the challenge of getting through the slower months of January through March. During the summer and fall months, they put money aside to cover at least two months of house payments, so they do not have to worry about making their mortgage payments in January or February. Usually, they can put together the funds needed to make one mortgage payment out of three months of even the slowest sales.

Slower months are also the perfect time to go back and call on every proposal that did not close during the previous year. It is not uncommon to make 2 or 3 sales per week by taking the time to contact all the customers over the past 12 months who did not make a purchase from you.

This is also a great time to make "cold calls" and share the benefits of installing a Reme Halo, Air Scrubber, or Phenomenal Aire to kill viruses and germ, to help eliminate dust and allergens, and to remove odors from a building. Many customers have 20-year-old ductwork that has never been cleaned. Often ductwork is undersized or poorly installed.

Some of the best places to make these "cold calls" are:
- Preschools
- Daycares
- Elementary Schools
- Dentist offices
- Medical offices
- Churches (especially for the children's areas)

- Senior Living facilities

Any place that has a lot of young children or older adults in closer proximity where germs are easily spread, is a great prospect to purchase these products. At the same time, getting your foot in the door opens the opportunity to add the facility to your maintenance program and to review the age of their equipment, and possibly to offer an "off-season" deal.

Cold calls deserve the highest commission rate of all. These calls usually cost the company little or no marketing money or other expenses. It is not uncommon for growing companies to offer 10-12% commissions on these sales. This may seem like a high percentage to pay, but, remember these kinds of sales often occur during your slowest season when cash flow is critical.

By offering a higher reward on cold calls (self-generated sales) you will motivate your sales team to keep the income funnel open so that you do not have to borrow money to make payroll. Remember that anything you do to avoid digging a financial hole during slow months is probably going to pay big dividends when business picks back up. Sometimes just breaking even is a win during your slowest two months of the year.

Cash flow is king.

Installation Pay

The sales price is one factor in whether you make a solid profit on equipment sales. However, the cost of installation is another significant factor in the profitability of your replacement sales. The old school way of paying installers is to pay them an hourly wage for installing equipment.

Have you ever noticed that an installation job that begins on a Monday or a Wednesday can often roll over into the next day? For some odd reason it can be a challenge for some installers to complete the installation in a single day. However, let me ask you this. How many times have you seen the same guys start an installation on Friday morning and be finished by 4:00 or 4:30 on the same day?

This example is a perfect description of why paying your installers on an hourly basis is a poor decision. You want your installers to care more than you about doing the job well and finishing on the same day. How can you achieve this? Pay your installers for the completed job rather than by the hour.

When you pay your installers for completing the work in a timely manner, they will make more money and also have more time for their family. They are less likely to cost you overtime as well. If you were an installer, which scenario below would you prefer?

Scenario #1 – Hourly pay of $30
Two guys work 8 hours each and are both paid $240 for the day.

Scenario #2 – Pay for work $250 for furnace - $250 for condenser - $150 for coil and line set.
Two guys work 8 hours each and at the end of the day they split $650 for a daily pay of $325.

In scenario #2, you do not pay the guys more if they roll the work over into the second day. They are paid for completing the job. However, you will be surprised how often the same two guys now finish their install jobs by 3:30 or 4:00 instead of working until 5:00 and still having some work undone. As long as you have work for them, your installers will become more efficient and actually increase the quality of their install work.

Another successful idea for keeping your installers motivated is a quarterly bonus program for installers. Each installer earns points for every successful install based on behaviors that you consider to be a priority.
- No callbacks on installs for the next 30 days.
- Installs completed in one day.
- Customer reviews received
- Add-on air quality equipment, water filtration, whole home surge protection etc.
- At least one customer referral for family, friends, neighbors
- Yard sign permission from the customer

At the end of each quarter, you tally each installer's points, and each installer is rewarded a bonus based on their percentage of the total points earned. The best part is that the bonus costs you NOTHING.

The way you fund the bonus pool for the installers is to add $50 to the price of every replacement or equipment sales. This $50 accrues in the install bonus pool for the quarter. If a call back occurs and the installer/s take care of it, they do not lose points. If a service tech is required to handle the call back, the $50 is transferred from the installer pool to the service department (at the end of the month, you simply count service callbacks on installations and tally the amount for a one-time transfer.) The installers lose points for that install.

Let's say you have two install teams, and they average six installs a week during the slow months. This would equal $3900 to be split out according to the points that your 4 installers earned. Some installers will receive a bonus over $1,000. In busy months, you may average as many as ten installs or more each week. This would equate as much as $6500 to be distributed at the end of a busy quarter.

Now let me ask you this. Do you think your competition is doing this? Do you think you could attract some quality installers with the potential of a quarterly bonus of $1,000 to $2,000 which would come their way four times a year? Do you think your installers would have a better Christmas for their family and maybe better vacations with a quarterly bonus?

When you can incentivize your installers to be more effective and at the same time to increase their efficiency, you stand to become more profitable. You will also know exactly how much to charge for each install when you build your pricing and you will not have to worry about overtime for installers, unless you ask them to work on a weekend. This program has worked for dozens of contractors, and it will work for you just as well.

What about your slowest months, when there are not as many jobs to install? How do you keep from losing your installers? First, when you begin to implement this total process, your sales are going to increase, so this problem is greatly diminished. When your installs get backed up, your techs slow down or stop selling new jobs. I have seen this over and over.ß

Breaking even in a slow month is a success

Still, there will be those weeks where very little is on the install board. So, what can you do to make sure your installers have work to do? One suggestion is to designate one or two weeks for building and facility rejuvenation during the slow times.

Paint, repair, and remodel your facilities to better meet your needs. Build or improve your training room. Buy and remodel a house or a small commercial space for rent. Your installers can do these projects and you will not be paying them to just sit in the warehouse nor will you need to send them home. They have bills to pay, so keep them busy.

When you keep your guys busy you will keep your guys. Men need to stay busy AND they need the security of having steady work. If you do not pay attention to these issues, you will soon have a group of negative thinking and poorly motivated workers.

Keep your guys busy and you will keep your guys.

Slow months are part of just about every business cycle. You need to expect slow months and have a plan in place for these times. Why not take advantage of a slower month to refurbish an "income producing" property such as a new rental property? This is a good time to teach your installers about buying their own rental properties to prepare for their future retirement income as well. You can build your own retirement income and be an example to your employees as well.

Takeaways from this chapter.

- *Do not raise prices by adding 10% to your old prices.*

- *Do not have low prices. Have high value.*

- *Keep pricing simple.*

- *Educate homeowners and they will buy better solutions.*

- *A cheap repair may be the most expensive thing you do to a homeowner.*

- *Let the customer pay the sales commission.*

- *Cash flow is king.*

- *Breaking even is a slow month is a success*

- *Keep your guys busy and you will keep your guys.*

Chapter 10
Plan Your Profits

What do you consider a reasonable net profit for all the time, energy, and challenges that you face each year in business? How much net profit makes the risk worthwhile? What is a fair price for running a business, owning and maintaining vehicles, making weekly payroll, funding a marketing plan, and overseeing daily operations?

These are tough questions, aren't they? Some of you probably would prefer just to ignore these kinds of questions. However, trying to ignore the issue of profit in your business is like ignoring your doctor's warning about your cholesterol, being overweight, high blood pressure, or poor food choices. At some point you would consider a person to be irresponsible if they continued with bad behaviors after being warned of an impending stroke or heart attack, right?

So why do so many owners ignore the issue of net profit? I actually had an owner tell me that his goal was to have zero net profit so that he did not have to pay any income tax. I don't think he even realized that he was saying he wanted to work all year and be financially broke to avoid taxes. This means his business is worth zero, so he can never sell it to anyone. A business has no value without a net profit.

If he earned no net profit, he has no capital to fund the start-up of a new year. My guess is he borrows money to make payroll in the first quarter of a new year. Believe me, this is not a good way to run a business.

Did you know that a non-profit organization needs to earn approximately 10% profit over and above their budgeted expenses in order to have capital to operate and grow in a new year? If non-profits are striving for 10% net profit, how can you be satisfied with anything less? Hopefully, you are not running a non-profit residential service business.

In reality, some owners are managing their business as if it were a non-profit organization. They likely do not even realize this is what they are doing. Do you think most owners had an opportunity to attend business school before they started their own business? No.

There are far more "accidental" owners in the world of residential service contractors than trained business leaders. However, you do NOT have to remain in this mode. I have a PhD with a concentration in business management. Let me show you the way to be more profitable.

I coach and train owners to develop a business growth model that achieves at least 2 of the following 3 items each year:
- Grow revenues by at least $500k if revenue is less than $3 million annually and grow by at least $1 million if annual revenues are over $3 million.
- Double the net profit if it is less than 5%
- Increase the net profit if it is over 10%… with a final net profit target of up to 25%

Focus on growing your business, not avoiding taxes.

Once you have a healthy net profit, there are many ways to protect your net profit, reinvest your net profit, or expense your net profit as a dividend and avoid your business paying excessive taxes. The goal should be to grow your business, NOT avoid taxes. Make sure you are aiming for the right target.

Understand your Profit/Loss Statement.

Another huge failure for HVAC residential contractors is their inability to receive a P&L statement in a timely manner, and/or their inability to understand the "financial story" the P&L statement is telling them.

I have never worked with a non-profit organization that did not provide a monthly report on budgeted expenses, income, and a report on the financial balance. In fact, it is exactly because money is often tight in a non-profit organization that they track their expenses and revenues so closely.

If you cannot get an accurate P&L report by the 5th to 7th day of a new month, then your process is broken. Would you take your family on a trip in a car with no speedometer or gas gauge? How big of a risk would you be taking? Would you possibly encounter a few surprises and have some negative outcomes…such as speeding tickets, running out of gas, etc.?

Even worse, what if you were to drive a car with a working gas gauge and speedometer and then deliberately choose to ignore them. You will likely encounter the same kinds of problems.

You must make it a priority to have an accurate P&L for review by the 5th to 7th of each month. Then you need to learn how to read it so that you can understand the story it is telling you. Reviewing a P&L is a simple 4 step process. A good P&L report has five key components.

These sections are described below with dollars and percentages for each major section of the P&L:
1) Income from Sales & Service
2) COGS (Cost of Goods Sold – Labor & Materials)
3) Gross Profit (Money to cover operating costs)
4) Operating Expenses
5) Net Profit (Profit remaining before taxes)

These suggestions are for a basic, easy to understand, quick to review P&L statement. In order to be able to "read" the financial story that your P&L is telling, you must know a few more details first.

The first section of your P&L should provide a breakdown of your revenue. This should include residential service, maintenance, commercial service, commercial maintenance, HVAC replacement sales, generator sales, water heaters, etc.

HVAC equipment sales should have a set price limit that is slightly higher than the cost of a cost of a coil replacement (only items over $3500). Coils and condenser replacements should normally be included in sales revenues. For plumbing equipment sales include water heaters and water filters, water softeners, etc. For electrical this category includes panel changeouts, generators, pool equipment, etc.

The second section of your P&L should be represented by your COGS which includes the following items:
- Equipment costs
- Materials & supplies costs
- Parts for service
- Parts for maintenance
- Labor for service

- Labor for install
- Subcontractors
- Equipment rental
- Commissions to salespeople

Essentially, any cost that is directly tied to completing your work in the field, should be included in COGS.

The third section of your P&L is your Gross Profit. This is the percentage and amount of gross profit, before you pay your operating expenses (overhead) for the month.

The fourth section of your P&L is your operating expenses which includes your advertising, vehicle costs, facility costs, office and manager costs, all insurance costs, utilities, training, and any other cost that is part of operating the business that is not directly part of completing a repair or equipment replacement in the field.

The fifth section of your P&L is your Net Profit. The goal is to be at 10% or higher and to increase your net profits every year.

A useful method for organizing your P&L to be able to spot trends is to follow the steps below in printing your report.

1 – Revenues and expenses by month for the entire year, with the most current month being in the farthest column to the right just before the YTD totals column.

2 – Financials report by each major source of revenues and expenses so that you can see the natural patterns that emerge. Some will be consistent, and others will vary month by month.

3 – Revenues and expenses for the same period YTD last year in the column immediately after your current YTD column.

The P&L is a snapshot of the health of your business.

It is not uncommon for a business to have one or two years of fantastic growth and profits, followed by a year of stabilizing revenues and profits, followed by another year of growth with higher capital costs and lower profits. However, it does NOT have to be this way.

There are some revenue stages where your capital expenses will increase significantly, thus lowering your net profits. You must make the strategic decision to grow "through" these stages to reach the next level of profitable business operations.

Some clients budget and replace 1/3 of their computers every year. Thus, they do not have a huge expense for new computers every 3 or 4 years. This means their computer systems work efficiently and effectively because none of their equipment is older than 3 years old. Simply replace some computers every year as a normal part of your operating process and you will save lots and lots of time, energy, and money with better human performance as well.

Clients can do the same thing with their vehicles by replacing one or two vehicles every year or every two years, depending on the number of vehicles they are operating. By putting this major expense into their regular operations, they are seldom hit with a huge expense of having to buy a new vehicle unexpectedly.

HINT: They keep the old vehicles as "stand by" vehicles and do not trade them in on any purchases of new vehicles.

What is a reasonable Cost of Goods Sold (COGS)?

What is the "average" cost of goods and services for a residential service company? What is a good target for COGS for a healthy company with a net profit over 10%?

Plenty of service companies have P&L statements with COGS over 60% This quickly tells us a few things:
- Net profit is likely less than 10%
- The equipment sales ratio to service calls is probably low
- Labor costs to sales revenue is probably high
- Equipment prices are likely too low and/or they are paying too much for the equipment they install.

COGS is controlled by your management efforts. COGS, especially the labor cost, is more likely an issue caused by management decisions than by your employees. Good management strategies and solid operational practices can keep COGS within an acceptable range, which is between 50% to 55%. Some clients are as low as 45% on their COGS and these clients are very profitable.

Client strategies for managing costs include using scorecards, incentive compensation, and many of the practices reviewed in this book. The better your plan, your tools, and your practices, the better your net profits.

The net profit is a reflection of the management team.

Gross Profit

An acceptable gross profit is typically above 45%, with the ideal goal of 55%. The reason is that operations costs for a service business are often in the range of 35%, which leaves only 10% for your net profit if the gross margin is 45%.

If operations costs are higher than 35%, then you must create a gross profit that is higher than 45% if you want to have double digit net profits. How do you achieve this? You must increase prices and manage technician hours.

It is plain and simple. In addition, operating costs including administration and office staff must be managed well to keep operating costs below 35% of sales.

Right now, some of you are thinking like a technician and not a business owner. You might be thinking things like:
- Customers won't pay more
- I will lose customers to my competition
- My competition will eat me alive
- People can shop on the internet to find cheaper prices
- People are going to call around and find someone cheaper

The answer to each of these questions is likely to be "yes" sometimes, but for what percentage of customers? You see, most customers do not remember what they paid for their last service repair. They do not have the convenience of time to shop around for service prices. I know that I don't.

Most people don't have the time or inclination to call to your competition. Others would not have called you if they knew how to replace the part such as DIYers (do it yourselfers) who try to fix problems themselves and then call you when they screw things up. Finally, most folks don't want to call around to save $20 or so on a repair. They want to get service from a company that is honest, respectful, and prompt.

The real problem is that you probably have not made a real connection with enough of your customers. Let me ask you this question. If I surveyed your customers, would the top 50-60% say they appreciate your company, they like your company, or they LOVE your company?

Appreciate = Average
Like = Good
LOVE = Excellent

If you only see and communicate with a customer 1-2 times a year, they *might* like you. If you communicate with a customer less than every 12 months, it is reasonable to say they probably think you are average. You are not doing anything more than any other service company has done to keep in touch with them.

What do companies do differently that make customers LOVE them? They provide extra value at no extra cost. For instance:
- Monthly text reminders to change your filter
- Monthly tips on making your home more energy efficient and ways to protect your home from damage
- Information on new technology advances

- Thank you cards on the anniversary of your becoming a customer or member of your maintenance club program
- Monthly coupons for friends and family

Notice that none of these items actually ASK you to spend money. This kind of communication is focused on saving money…for the customer and their friends and family.

The truth about price increases is that you need to increase service prices at least twice a year – every 6 months. By the end of the year, most or all items have been increased by 10-20%. If you did not increase your service prices last year by 10%, you are likely at least 25-30% underpriced right now.

Operational Expenses

As you read a few paragraphs back, most companies aim to keep operations below 35%. Now if you have a growth strategy, then you have already committed to 6 to 10% for marketing.

This means you have only 25 to 29% available for total operations which includes insurance, vehicles, facilities, office staff, manager salaries, personnel benefits, computers and office equipment, office supplies, etc.

Pay off your vehicles and other debts. During the summer, reinvest some of your profit into reducing your debts. Sometimes it is smarter to buy a good used truck and replace an engine than to owe $65,000 to $70,000 for a new truck. Any vehicle you have is going to need repairs. It is cheaper to repair a vehicle that does not have a monthly payment.

Are you using a GPS system to track the maintenance on your vehicles? A good GPS software will tell you when it is time for to change the oil, transmission fluid, brake fluid, engine coolant, rotate tires, etc. Some systems will also warn you if your technician is braking too hard or driving too fast.

Do not rely on your technicians to maintain your vehicles. A good technician has more important things to focus on. Would you rather your techs average over $300 per service call, get 30 to 40% of customers to write a positive review, sign up 8 to 10 new club members a month, and flip one or two replacement leads a week?

Then you need a better plan for getting the oil changed and checking the tires on your trucks. Don't rely on your techs for mechanical maintenance.

By the way, have you looked inside of their truck? Judging by the messiness that I usually see, I am not going to trust that the technician will maintain the mechanical aspects of the truck any better than they treat the inside of the truck. Putting this responsibility on your technicians is poor management and likely foolish if you want to avoid unnecessary repair costs.

The topic of incentives is common for technicians and sales, but it is amazing how few companies have an incentive program for the top of their business funnel – the office team.

Do you realize that the average call is worth an average of $700 to $1,000? Booking one extra call each week has the potential to bring in more revenue than you pay a good CSR in a week.

What are you doing to make sure your CSRs and office team are producing at their top level? How much effort and buy-in does your office team have to make sure your business meets the revenue goals EVERY WEEK? What makes them care about assigning the *right technician* for every call? If there is nothing in the way of incentives for your office team, I can guarantee there are plenty of weeks that you miss your weekly revenue goal by more than $1,000.

You want your office team to "care" about hitting the weekly goal. In fact, you want to have a program in place, so they care MORE about hitting the weekly goal than the owner/s.

Your office team should care MORE than you about hitting the weekly revenue goal.

Achieve a Double-Digit Net Profit

- Focus
- Caring
- Focus

Nothing great happens without a lot of planning, but mostly the results are due to focus. Just about anybody can come up with a pretty good plan or possibly even a great plan. It is the few who stay focused week by week who usually achieve the initial target goals.

FOCUS is king in business! Have you ever driven a vehicle that had a broken or missing speedometer? Well, I can tell you that it is pretty easy to keep it between 20-30 miles per hour, just by guessing. That is what many, many business owners are doing. Their business grows slowly because this feels comfortable, and they can manage it by doing a lot of guessing.

However, try driving a vehicle and keeping it between 50-60 mph or even better, try to keep it between 65-75 without being able to view the speedometer. It is a LOT harder than you may think.

For a business to sustain continued healthy growth, you need key monitors in place to track your income goals, your gross profit, your expenses, and your net profit EVERY week. If you only see a P&L 10-15 days after the month is over, how can you know whether you are managing your business to a healthy net profit? You will be almost halfway through the next month before you see lagging feedback for the previous month.

Every week you need to view your balance sheet, income statement, and your business scorecard so that you KNOW exactly where you are and how much more you need in sales to make the month a success.

Have you noticed how often an NFL running back or quarterback gets exactly enough yardage for a 1st down? Can you picture a player struggling for that one extra yard just to get past the first down marker? This is the reason they have the markers for 1st down on both sidelines. It is easy to see. It is a constant reminder that progress is measured 10 yards at a time, not just by scoring touchdowns.

Your annual profit is measured a week and a month at a time. These are your 1st down markers, and you have to put out the effort to make sure you consistently score 1st downs long before you score a touchdown and achieve your net profit goal.

You cannot have a healthy profit if you use a P&L halfway into the next month as your primary profit monitor.

A healthy business has a breakeven number and a true breakeven number for every month. A smart business owner makes adjustments to exceed the breakeven EVERY month. Every time your business doesn't surpass your breakeven, you dig a hole for the following month which pushes your next month's true breakeven even farther out.

This is a reason so many companies fail to achieve a double-digit net profit. The hole that is created by the 1st quarter of subpar revenue leaves a BIG gap to close for the 2nd quarter. By the time the 3rd quarter is finished you usually have a decent profit, which is diminished by subpar revenues in the 4th quarter. Sometimes just breaking even is a win, because you have not dug a hole that you have to overcome in the next month.

How do you make sure you break even every month? First, you need to know your monthly operational costs. Then divide your operational costs, by your gross profit percent. This is your breakeven or "broke even" number.

Example:
Operational costs: $55,000
Gross Profit %: 52%

$55,000 / 52% = $105,770

It will take $105,770 in revenues each month to leave enough gross profit to cover your operational costs.

So how much do you need to generate 10% net profit?

Multiply your "required revenue" amount of $105,770 by 10% and you get $10,577.

Add $10,577 to your operational costs and divide the new total by 52% once again.

Example:
Operational costs: $55,000 + $10,577 = $65,577
Gross Profit %: 52%

$65,577 / 52% = $126,110

Your business will provide you with over $10,000 in net profits each month when you book enough calls and sales to reach $126,110 in revenue sales.

Chapter 11
Build a Team of Rock Stars

Your Service Team

Your service department is vital to maintaining a steadily growing business. To maintain a solid base of satisfied customers, you should invest in coaching for your service team.

Your CSRs, dispatcher, and technicians all need training on a weekly or biweekly basis depending on the season and your scorecard results. It is best to build in some "breaks" or "time off" from training as well. Most people appreciate a small break from the routine every 6 weeks or so.

CSRs and dispatchers are like baseball pitchers or football quarterbacks. They set up each call. If they are not setting things up effectively, then you will not be able to put the points on the business scoreboard that you need to win.

What percentage of incoming calls are currently booked for service calls or sales proposals? Do you even know? If not, consider this. For every two calls that are not booked, you forfeit an amount that is a close equivalent to the entire weekly pay of your CSR or dispatcher. A good CSR/dispatcher books over 90% of all incoming calls. Until you are achieving this percentage, it makes no sense to throw more money at marketing. Make sure you are capturing a fair percentage of your incoming calls from marketing and current customers.

CSRs and dispatchers will do a much better job if they have a weekly target as well. Consider a bonus program that rewards your CSR/dispatcher every week that the company revenue goal is achieved. It does not have to be a big amount of money to make a very BIG difference.

Consider something like $50 per week and an additional $100 when the monthly revenue goal is achieved. You will be surprised how much more often you achieve your revenue goals.

Sending the "right technician" to each job is just as important as booking the "right calls". If you have no incentive for your CSR/dispatcher to give careful thought to how they assign calls, why should they pay special attention to this critical matter? Make it worth something to them. Putting a bonus program in place can turn a routine work environment into a fun and competitive culture.

Sustained success and business growth are the result of *good energy*, not hours worked. Do you want to pay your employees to "put in 8 hours" of time, or would you prefer to pay them for giving their best energy for 8 hours? Any reward system that keeps your team focused on achieving results for their own benefit will provide your business with the best possible opportunity for making a healthy profit.

Consider the following:

- When you miss your weekly revenue goal, how often do you fall short by more than a couple hundred dollars?
- When you have a service opportunity that may require upgrades or new equipment, do you care which technician is assigned to the call?

- If your technicians can see all their calls at the start of the day, are they going to be flexible when their assignments change?
- Will your techs be flexible to get dispatched across town for a high "opportunity call"?
- If you dispatch from home, are your technicians likely to have the same energy and appearance as they have on the days they meet at the office for training?
- When a call comes in, does your office have a triage system of 4-5 colors they use to schedule the call? Doing this makes it much easier to decide which technician to assign to a call when the time arrives.
- Are your technicians given a color code according to their skill level? Is this reviewed and updated on a quarterly basis? The more the CSR/dispatcher knows about a technician's skill level, the more effectively they can dispatch for profits!

Your technicians will perform with more focus and consistency if you create a compensation plan based on their performance. Having several levels of technicians also gives your team something to aspire to achieve.

Your level 1 technicians may only be capable of doing maintenance calls, while others are level 2 service technicians (they can do maintenance and basis service), or level 3 service technicians (they can diagnose and repair more service issues) or level 4 service technicians (they run most of the service calls on older equipment and they can sell new systems).

To qualify for a pay increase, you might list 6 or 7 work skills and behaviors and set targets to qualify before a tech can request a pay increase. If an employee knows what is required each year to qualify for more pay, most will adjust their behaviors accordingly. For example:

Team Standards

- Be on time and ready to work by 7:30 am
- Keep your truck clean, organized, and tidy
- Perform task(s) as assigned by dispatchers and/or manager
- Provide workmanship capable of meeting or exceeding our warranties

Customer Service:

- Maintain a customer satisfaction rate over 95%
- Wear floor savers while inside the home
- Keep the work area clean
- Use drop cloths while inside the home
- Clean-up after the work is done
- Inform the customer of any safety or code violations
- Communicate with the customer so that they have a clear understanding of the job
- Operate at all times with the utmost integrity

Revenue Standards:

- Call close rate over 80% for service calls in the field
- Average ticket over $350
- Monthly revenue goal over $25,000
- Minimum monthly revenue of $22,000
- Club conversion rate over 50%

Paperwork:

- Complete all work tickets while onsite
- Customer signatures on all paperwork
    - Review the inspection sheet with customer (get signature)
    - Provide 4 options with customer initials
- Turn in all work tickets with payment or payment information to the office daily
- Communicate with the dispatcher the job information required on EVERY call

Service Technicians

- Qualify to receive 5% on any invoice over $400 (up to $1000 max. = $40 max per invoice)
- Techs who produce $20,000 in revenue in a month will receive a 1% bump in ticket commission OR $250 BONUS after $20,000 and then $200 for every $5,000 over the $20,000 until the end of the month.

To Qualify for an Annual Raise

- $250,000 in Service & Maintenance
- $550,000 Total Revenue (includes leads flipped & sold)
- 100 Customer Reviews
- 100 Club Memberships Sold
- 500 Units Stickered
- Avg. Ticket over $325 for 10 of 12 months
- # Callbacks limited < 2% of calls run for 10 of 12 months

Maintenance Technicians who produce $10,000 in revenue in a month will receive a 1% bump in ticket commissions.

Techs receive a percentage if the average weekly invoice exceeds $200 as follows:
- >$200 avg. ticket for week = 2%
- >$225 avg. ticket for week = 3%
- >$250 avg. ticket for week = 4%

To Qualify for an Annual Raise
- $150,000 in Service & Maintenance
- $300,000 Total Revenue (includes leads flipped & sold)
- 100 Customer Reviews
- 100 of Clubs Sold
- 500 Units Stickered
- Avg. Ticket over $200 for 10 of 12 months
- 50 Accessories Sold

Installers respond in much the same way as technicians. Most good workers want to know what is expected of them, so they can deliver what is required and feel good about their work performance. Why would you not have a scoreboard for installers as well?

In fact, many contractors have a bonus/reward program for installers as well. It costs the contractor nothing to offer this. Consider that you could add a flat $100 to each system sale or $50 to a water heater or electric panel installation. Now, the installer will accrue $50 for every installation that is completed in a single day and which does not require a callback for at least 7 days (some contractors set this at 30 days with no callback).

These funds are paid as follows. At the end of each quarter, every installer is paid $25 to $50 per install that meets the company standards. If they complete an average of 3-4 installs per week, this can easily accrue to more than $2,000 per quarter. Now that's a nice bonus check!

How does this help your business? Well for one, think how difficult it would be for a good installer to leave you for someone else. They would be walking away from a much as $8,000 to $10,0000 a year in bonus pay.

Second, what about paying for the callbacks? Now you have a pool of funds to pay a technician if they have to run a callback on an install. Each installer forfeits their $50 for the install bonus and $100 is transferred into the service budget to pay the technician. You have created a set of "golden handcuffs" to help retain your installers, and you have created a safety net of funds to pay for install callbacks without giving up your profits.

These are only suggestions for your consideration. However, contractors who have adopted these standards have experienced more satisfaction with their technician performance, and their technicians have earned significantly more compensation by producing more revenue for the business.

Your Sales and Install Team

Most contractors set revenue goals for their sales team. Truthfully, this does not motivate most salespeople. They will tell you they try their best regardless, but that is not usually true either. They probably believe they are doing their best, but few people actually achieve their best without a clear target and a clear bonus or reward in place for achieving the target.

Most salespersons (comfort advisors, comfort specialists, service supervisors, etc.) like a challenge. They are in the field of sales because they enjoy the challenge and the rewards of closing a sale.

However, few start the month with a specific goal in mind for how many sales they intend to close. By creating clear targets for each quarter (based on the previous 3 years of actual sales data) you will actually give your sales team an awesome gift. You will be providing them with something to aim for and achieve. Make sure to have an adequate rewards system set up for those who exceed the target, as these are your most valuable employees on the sales team.

This reward may be as simple as increasing the sales commission by 2% for all sales over and above the goal each month. In this case, you are giving away almost nothing.

The true profitability of a sale increases 5 to 10-fold after you achieve your breakeven each month. Why not add a little incentive for your sales team to close even more sales in the last week of the month? This way your business can close out each month on a strong note instead of your team giving up and just going through the motions because they are tired.

Extra incentives give your best people more energy!

Your Office Team

What is the primary goal of your office team? The correct answer is NOT to answer the phone and book calls. The primary goal of your office team is to fill the service board with calls for your field team.

This may involve answering the phone for incoming calls, but it also includes making outgoing calls. A great office staff will book maintenance calls when the board is slow, but they will also call clients who have not contacted you in over a year. These are customers who you have served in the past and these are the easiest customers to reengage with the right kind of offer.

What kind of offer should you consider? Here are a few ideas:
- Try an air purification accessory for 30 days at no risk.
- Get their system cleaned and tested for a one-time low price
- Add surge protection for 40% off this month
- Free washer hose replacements with any repair or accessory upgrade
- $400 off a tankless water heater or $250 off a tank water heater
- $600 off an HVAC system or electric panel

When calls are slow, your office team needs to be ready to spring into action and make offers that will book calls. These offers need to be designed and prepared in advance. When you have a slow day, just pick one or two offers and hit the phones.

A good office team keeps the board booked with calls.

Your Management Team

What is the primary role of your management team? It is NOT to put out fires and organize everyone's day. Your managers must focus their personal energy on improving production, customer satisfaction, and execution of your processes.

The title "manager" can be misleading. Managers do not manage people. People naturally resist and detest being "managed." People respond to leadership.

So, your managers need to manage the business processes that increase performance, production, and profitability. Managers are your front-line drivers of success. They need to focus on meeting company goals and motivating their team members through positive interaction and communication.

If you want your managers to help keep your team focused, then you need to keep your managers focused on the business goals. If your managers have something to gain for leading their team to achieve your business goals, they are much more likely to be focused and productive.

When your business wins, everyone on the team should win in some personal way. When you keep your focus on making winners then success will find you naturally. Winners cannot help but become successful.

Make winners. Winners become successful.

Moving Big Rocks

What am I talking about? Big rocks are what you call the 5 biggest obstacles or challenges in each department of your business. Every manager needs to have a list of 4-5 Big Rocks to focus on moving in the right direction each year.

Sometimes, with enough focus, you can move all your rocks early enough in the year that you need to create a new list for the 3rd or 4th quarter of the year. This is great news! It means you are gathering momentum and making progress toward improving your business operations.

Smart business leaders know that 3 to 4 improvements each quarter will make a "massive" difference by the end of the year. When you move a few "Big Rocks" each quarter, you can make 12 or more major improvements in your business which will pay off Big Time.

Keep Winners on Your Team

Do you have a plan that creates "golden handcuffs" to retain your best employees? What am I talking about?

I am referring to a retirement account with offers a 100% return on the employee's investment. It's simple to set up and will pay you returns many times over. Consider a simple plan like this.

When you employee is paid, encourage them to put 4% or 5% of their paycheck into the retirement fund. Then your business matches the employee's contribution up to the 4% or 5% limit that you establish. Each year the employee remains, they get to keep 20% of your contributions.

Example of vesting:

1 year   = 20% vested
2 years = 40% vested
3 years = 60% vested
4 years = 80% vested
5 years =100% vested

Vested simply means, the employee may keep the percentage of company contributions equal to the percentage of their vested status. Getting "free money" with 100% return on their investment is about the best deal any employee can hope to receive. Now let's see that the market can do for the employee by investing in a matching retirement fund for 10 years.

If an employee earns $25 per hour and works a full 40 hours each week, their gross pay would be $1,000 and after taxes approximately $750. A small 4% contribution would be only $30 and with the company match that becomes $60. What will this look like after 10 years?

Let's say the employee is 25 years old. At age 35, their retirement account will have grown to over $75,000. At age 45, the account will be over $270,000. At age 55, their account will be as much as $780,000 and at age 65 their account will be worth over $2.2 million dollars! *

All this can be achieved at the rate of only $30 a week invested into a Roth IRA retirement account. The best part is that the entire account can be withdrawn tax free after age 65. That's right. The employee pays no taxes on their account because they invest their deposits from "after tax" dollars.

One more thought that seems almost crazy. Listen to this. If the employee only invested the $30 weekly for 10 years and then stopped, guess what their account would be worth at age 65? If they stopped investing any more of their weekly paycheck after 10 years, their account would still grow to over $1.7 million dollars! *

This is incredible right? The power of compound interest is almost unbelievable.

Convince your employees to stay and grow rich together!

*Investment growth is based on an average growth rate of 11% for the U.S. Market over the past 100 years.

Takeaways from this chapter

- *Extra incentives give your best people more energy!*

- *A good office team keeps the board booked with calls.*

- *Make winners. Winners become successful.*

- *Keep Winners on Your Team*

- *Convince your employees to stay and grow rich together!*

KEY CONCEPTS - Ready, Set, Read, & Grow!

- *Systems and solid strategies produce better results on a consistent basis.*

- *Profits are more important than revenues.*

- *You are in the marketing business.*

- *Sustained growth is never by accident.*

Chapter 12
Sustained Business Growth

What is the secret to growing your business?
Why do some owners seem to have the "magic touch" when it comes to business growth and others do not?

The answer is not as difficult as you might think. The secret is having a solid annual business plan for growth. The magic is knowing how to create a solid business plan that is appropriate for your business and for your community.

I strongly suggest that you consider two key resources if you are serious about growing your business. First, you need an experienced and proven guide. Do not let your pride get in the way. The best athletes and business CEOs in the world, have performance coaches. We all need someone who can give us an objective perspective and who is unafraid to challenge us on decisions that could potentially negatively impact our business.

Second, I suggest that you partner with a training organization that will challenge and sharpen the skills of your employees. Your best players are the ones who will benefit the most from training. Good training helps your team develop their personal systems and hone their skills for greater consistency. It helps establish benchmarks and tracks each person's results so they can get better and be more consistent.

Training allows a good coach to help you create bonus programs that reward performance AFTER your monthly breakeven has been achieved. This motivates your best employees, because they now have a target to aim for and a sense of personal pride and accomplishment each month when they achieve a bonus. People are more satisfied and committed to their organization when they have tangible proof they are doing well, being recognized, and being rewarded accordingly.

Coaching

You see, without benchmarks and monthly rewards, most jobs can become routine and boring. Employees begin to just go through the motions. They don't let it bother them when they lose a customer, fail to successfully book a call, or end up with invoices that fail to produce a fair profit for the company.

Whose fault is this? The responsibility for growth lies squarely on the shoulders of the person at the top. You are their coach. Whoever owns and manages the business is responsible to provide the training and coaching that your team needs to win.

At the time of writing, at the age of 42 years, Tom Brady had more wins in NFL football than any other quarterback who managed to play until age 40.

Tom Brady (age 42) – 244 wins
Brett Favre (age 41) – 186 wins
Drew Brees (age 40) – 164 wins
Warren Moon (age 44) – 102 wins
Vinnie Testaverde (age 44) – 92 wins
Mark Brunell (age 41) – 83 wins
Earl Morrall (age 42) – 63 wins
Steve DeBerg (age 44) – 54 wins
Doug Flutie (age 43) – 38 wins
Peyten Manning (age 39) – 186 wins

More interesting though is the fact that Tom Brady and his coach, Bill Belichick, partnered for more than double the wins of all other quarterbacks who were playing at the age of 42. Whether you cheer for Tom Brady or not, you must admit their system delivered consistent results for much longer than any other NFL quarterback in history.

Systems and solid strategies produce better results.

Training

What are some of the key items that you need to implement for a solid business growth plan? Here are some of the most essential items that business owners focus on when they build their annual growth plan.

1) Number of service calls per month (estimate based on past 3 years)
2) Average invoice per service call (set an achievable target and train to it)
3) Number of installs per month (as a % of service calls)
4) Average invoice per install (set an achievable target and train to hit it)
5) Number of maintenance calls per month (estimate based on past 2 years)
6) Average invoice per maintenance call (add-on sales)
7) Average maintenance fees per month (estimate based on maintenance club members)

These are seven easy-to-measure benchmarks. In fact, these are the foundation of your service business. If you do not set these targets in advance, then you are not steering or guiding your business. Instead, you will tend to become reactive and pulled and pushed in many directions based on the "crisis of the moment". This is no way to manage an effective business. You cannot grow your business successfully if you are constantly in "firefighting" mode.

What processes do you need to have in place in order to achieve your goals?

1 – Clear targets for every employee to achieve
2 – Incentives for your employees to achieve the weekly and monthly revenue necessary to hit your "true breakeven"
3 – Weekly scoreboard to update employees on their progress toward achieving a monthly bonus
4 – A trainer who offers a "third party" perspective to your team
5 – Coach each player according to their personal needs and motivators
6 – Business scorecard to help you focus on the essential areas of production and growth (see the example provided)
7 – Marketing plan that successfully addresses all four key levels of branding and customer acquisition

The seven items above are the basics for EVERY business owner who consistently grows his business and keeps it highly profitable. Now, you need to always remember the following key point.

Profits are more important than revenues.

* Breakeven is the point at which the business has made enough money to pay all recurring monthly expenses and make the payroll, but not yet produce a profit.

** True Breakeven is the point at which the business has surpassed the breakeven point and produced enough funds to pay towards loans and achieve at least 10% net profit.

Be Profitable

If you grow your revenues but do not increase your profits, all you are doing is creating more work for yourself and your team. Most owners love to talk about their total revenue production or how much sales increased for the year.

This means nothing…unless it is followed with an honest comment on their net profit (EBITA). It is better to have a $2 million business with 12% net profit ($240,000), than a $5 million business with a 4% net profit ($200,000). In business, size doesn't matter as much as profitability.

Is it realistic to grow every year? Yes, it is critical that your business plan include growth every year. If you only grow 10%, then you are basically in a holding pattern. Inflation will eat up at least 3% of your growth and vendor price increases can easily eat up another 6-7% of your growth.

Business Scorecards

A business scorecard provides measures of how well your business is working. Think of KPIs as the gauges on a truck's dashboard. They quickly warn you of hazards to your growth.

Business Scorecard
The 12 KPIs for a Profitable Business

	KPIs	Poor	Fair	Good	Great
1	Tech Revenue per Hour	< $110	$110 - $115	$115 - 125	> $125
2	Service Average Ticket	< $275	> $275	> $300	> $325
	Maintenance Average Ticket	< $150	$150 - $175	$175 - $200	> $200
	Install Average Ticket	< $7000	$7000 - $7999	$8000 - $9499	> $9500
3	Tech Closing Rate *(Repair, Lead, Club)*	< 80%	80% - 84.9%	85 - 89.9%	> 90%
	Daily Calls per Service Technician	6	5	4	3
4	Service Truck Ranking	< 5.5	5.5 - 6.9	> 7	> 8
5	Company Revenue per Employee	< $11,000	$11k - $12.9k	$13k - 14.9k	> $15k
6	COGS %	> 55%	53 - 55%	50 - 52.9%	< 50%
7	Net Profit %	< 7%	7% - 9.9%	10% - 15%	> 15%
8	CSR Booking Rate	< 80%	80% - 84.9%	85 - 90%	> 90%
9	Leads per Tech (Monthly)	< 1	2 - 3.9	4 - 5.9	> 6
10	Service Calls to Install Jobs Ratio	< 10%	10 - 12.49%	12.5% - 16.49%	> 16.5%
	Service Calls to Install Jobs Number	> 10	8 - 9	6 - 7	< 5
11	Maintenance Club Closing Rate	< 45%	45 - 50%	51 - 59%	> 60%
	Maintenance Club Members	< 750 members	750 - 849	850 - 1000	> 1000 members
12	Customer Reviews	< 20% Reviews	20% - 29.9%	30% - 35%	> 35% Reviews

KPIs are super powerful and informative. The 12 KPIs above are very effective. While you may be familiar with some of them, it is possible that some of these KPIs are new to you.

1. Tech Revenue per Hour is calculated by dividing a technicians' revenue by the number of hours in a work period. This is typically calculated for each week and then finally for the month.

2. The Average Tickets – Service, Maintenance, Install. These are calculated by dividing the revenue for each area by the number of invoices submitted in Service, Maintenance, or for Replacements.

3. Tech Closing Rate is calculated by dividing the number of demand service calls that are "money calls" by the total number of demand service calls the tech ran. A money call is a call with at least

one repair over and above the dispatch fee. A call with just a dispatch fee does not count as a revenue call.

4. Tech Power Ranking is calculated by dividing the total revenue generated by a technician (includes service, maintenance, and leads for equipment that is sold) by the total hours submitted for a work period.

5. Company Revenue per Employee is calculated by dividing the total company revenue per month by the total number of full-time employees. Most part time employees count as 0.5.

6. COGS % is calculated by dividing the COGS dollar amount by the total revenue for a month, quarter, or year.

7. Net Profit % is calculated by dividing the net dollar amount by the total sales revenue for a month, quarter, or year.

8. CSR Booking Rate is calculated by subtracting vendor calls, tech calls, etc. from the total incoming call number. Then divide the number of calls booked by the number of incoming calls that were a possible service request.

9. Leads per Tech is the number of replacement leads set up by a technician per month. This can vary by season.

10. Service-to-Install Ratio is calculated by dividing the number of service calls for a month by the number of installs sold during the month.

11. Club Member Closing Rate is calculated by dividing the number of club members sold by the number of service calls booked for customers who were not club members.

12. Customer Reviews Rate is calculated by the number of customer reviews received for a month by the number of calls run by a technician.

Over my years of working with residential service contractors, it has become apparent that too few owners have a dashboard in place so they can spot trouble as soon as it starts. By the time most owners realize they have a problem in an area, the behaviors and patterns have been festering for weeks or months.

When business owners begin to track these 12 areas, they discover their business grows faster. They stay on top of the business health indicators. When a KPI changes, it is usually due to the behavior of your team OR it could be due to very low or very high call volume.

In either case, it is the owner's and managers' responsibility to monitor, and manage call volume, call assignments, and call results. If you are not using a business scorecard, how can you be confident that you are tracking your business health on a daily and weekly basis?

Growth Plans

Most healthy businesses plan to grow by at least 15-20% annually. A healthy business CANNOT remain static. A year of "no growth" in business revenue means your business is declining. A business is a living organism, and it must be growing, or it is slowly dying. There is no in between.

The average business must add approximately 30% new customers each year. Remember that some customers will move, some will divorce, some will die, some will simply not need or use your services for a year.

Many contractors think they are in the home services business. This is a short-sighted view of your actual business. A healthy business owner sees things differently. You see, you are really in the *marketing business*. The products and services that you market are for residential home services.

You are in the marketing business.

Planning for growth is beneficial in many ways. It keeps you focused on continuous improvement, which prevents you from becoming lethargic or lazy in managing your business. When a business is growing, the owner and managers are most often focused on executing a business plan.

Growth can be accidental. Sustained growth is never by accident. Success comes as the result of a well-executed plan. Planning to grow also means that you must stay focused on your marketing and branding strategy.

The average company must replace approximately 30% of your customers every year. This may be due to the customer moving out of your service area or not utilizing your services in the following year. Nevertheless, you will still need customer sales. This requires a continual focus on customer acquisition. In order to grow, you must have a plan to increase your share of the market.

Sustained growth is never by accident.

You may find that purchasing smaller companies is an easy way to gain market share. Sometimes, you can purchase the customer list and phone number from another owner who is tired of running his or her business and just wants a way out.

Other business purchases may provide you with more vehicles, additional technicians (do not plan on all of them staying or performing at the level of your current team), and even a new location if their building is in another service area.

Warning: never purchase another business without hiring a trained "business evaluator" who is very familiar with your industry. A realtor or a banker are NOT equipped in most cases to properly evaluate the real value of a business that you are considering for purchase. Seldom is a business worth what the owner is asking.

*The rare exception is when the business owner has utilized the seven key items listed above and can prove their net worth has increased annually over the previous three years.

Fast Growth vs. Steady Growth

Fast growth is exciting. It is also dangerous and precipitous. The business can crash or decline just as fast as it grew. Fast growth requires a constant influx of new employees. New employees require more attention and training. It will take extra time to get them trained to the level of your other employees. New employees have less commitment to the long-term health of your business, and they may leave for greener pastures more often and more easily.

Fast growth is often due to a large increase in installations which are your most profitable and highest revenue services. However, solid and steady growth is built on a foundation of a growing base of service and maintenance customers. These are the people who will seek your services year after year.

Replacements and installs are highly profitable, but then these customers may not need your services for several years to come. You will have to find new customers next year to make up for the installations that you do this year.

REMEMBER:
A healthy business is built on the foundation of a solid base of service customers. Without a solid foundation of service customers, you can end up building an installation company that resembles the leaning tower of Pisa. The slightest hiccup in the economy may be enough to topple your company.

A healthy business is based on service customers.

Slow growth can be just as challenging as fast growth. If your business is not growing steadily, then your team will slip into complacency more easily. They will not pay attention to the business scoreboard or their weekly and monthly scores. If growth is too slow, it can be hard to achieve momentum and without momentum, it is very difficult to maintain a healthy return on your investment of time and expenses.

Steady growth is the best growth.

Make Your Business Recession Proof

Is it possible to build a recession proof business? Yes, of course. Remember, that if you are in the residential home services market, you are serving the largest market in the world. Most people want to take care of their homes. This is the biggest investment they have made.

Not only is this true, but people want to be comfortable. Most people will not tolerate being too hot or too cold for more than a day at a time. They are going to call somebody to take care of their problem. Why shouldn't that somebody be your team?

This doesn't change in a recession. In fact, personal comfort is one of the items that homeowners will spend money on, regardless of the economy. Now a homeowner may be less likely to replace their equipment during a slow economy, but this means they are likely to need your services more often if they decide to repair their older systems which will likely have more problems down the road.

Build a Strong Service Base

This brings us back to the importance of having a very good maintenance club program. There are some key items that make a maintenance plan attractive and valuable to a homeowner. You must know that unless the value of the club program exceeds the price of the club program, people are not going to sign up easily. Therefore, provide so much value in your club program that it becomes a "no brainer" for customers to join.

Tips for your Maintenance Club.

1. Make your maintenance program a rewards club, or savings club, or comfort club. People are comfortable with joining these kinds of programs with other places of business (airline points, retail rewards/points, discounts). However, people DO NOT like to sign contracts or agreements. Make it easy to join and have a straightforward easy process for them to opt out if they do not believe they are getting the value they expect.

2. Train your team to present the value of your club program before they discuss any discounts that it provides.
   - 9 out of 10 breakdowns can be avoided with regular maintenance
   - Most equipment can last up to 30% longer if it is maintained professionally
   - Club members tend to spend 15% up to 32% less on utilities than homeowners who are not in a maintenance club.
   - Manufacturer warranties remain intact with proof of maintenance (without proof of maintenance most manufacturers void the original warranty)
   - Priority Service is given to club members. If their neighbor is a club member, they will get serviced first on the hottest or coldest days or after hours or on weekends.

3. Sign up customers immediately after showing them how much they will save as a club member.
   - Most maintenance club programs waive the dispatch/diagnostic fee if the customer does a repair AND joins the maintenance club

- Most maintenance club programs provide a 10%, 15%, or 20% discount off current repairs if the customer joins at the time of service
- Many maintenance club programs offer a discount on the purchase of new equipment or even better allow the customer to accrue "company cash" each year which can grow to a maximum of $500 or $1000 or $2000 toward the purchase of new equipment, depending on the level of purchase they make.

4. Maintenance club programs are your best customer retention tool. This helps you get the most return on your marketing dollars spent. The maintenance club is NOT expected to produce massive amounts of cash or profit by itself. Instead, it is a key part of your overall profit strategy.

5. Monthly maintenance payment programs have a higher retention rate than maintenance club programs that require a large annual payment. If the value of the club program was presented properly, most homeowners will remain in your club program for years, especially due to the priority service, protecting their equipment warranty, and to make things last as long as possible.

Be Debt Free

Your true breakeven will be much lower, if you have no debt or loans to pay off in your business. You may be thinking, well that would be nice but.... Wait just a minute! It is not only possible. This is realistic if you are willing to do a little work.

A debt-free business is more profitable.

You probably know that your business can lease your trucks from a separate company that you own which can charge a fair market rate for providing the vehicles and maintaining them. This helps stabilize your monthly expenses for vehicles.

The same is true for your building and utilities. You can own a separate business that leases your building (including utilities) in order to provide a steady expense for your contracting business.

Many business owners have a business that provides their furniture, computers, and even tools for their contracting business. This is another way to stabilize your monthly expenses.

Some may be thinking, what if I finish the year with a big profit and now have a large tax burden. This could be true for a business owner without a strategic plan, but not for YOU. So how will you handle the eventual pile of profits that you accrue?

Never fear paying taxes because you made a healthy profit.

Here are some suggestions on the best use of your profit:

1 – Pay off all loans including your building, trucks, equipment, and purchase all new computers and office equipment for your business every 4 years.

2 – Invest in commercial "rental space" and put your profits into remodeling and refurbishing the new space. Improvements are a tax write-off, as is the labor that your team can provide during the slower months of February and March.

3 – Invest in a company retreat that your team members could use once a year for a family getaway

4 – Invest in a "vacation program" that provides 5-10 weeks of vacation time each year. Set up requirements for employees to qualify. Now they can choose locations across the U.S. to take their family for a week of vacation. Your CPA can show you how to set this up as a business expense.

5 – Invest in a company retirement program such as an IRA or insurance annuity plan which can grow and provide significant benefits to employees who stay with the business and become fully vested

Now these are just a few ideas, and a good tax lawyer or knowledgeable financial advisor can provide you with additional options - *if they are good at what they do*. Remember that all financial advisors and tax attorney are not equal.

HINT: A CPA is not trained to help you save on taxes. Their goal is to help you avoid as much risk as possible, so they work very hard to make sure you pay any and all possible taxes that may put you at risk.

The point is this – why not protect your profits and make them work for you, rather than just pay massive amounts of taxes or forego the accumulation of profits altogether. Didn't you get into business to make a profit? Then let's start achieving this goal!

Maintain Cash Reserves

People often ask how much they should have in cash reserves. Well, this depends on lot of factors, but let's keep it as simple as possible. You need enough in cash reserves to pay your projected payroll and operating expenses for 2-3 months (as if no revenues were created). Now realistically, are you going to ever experience 3 months with no revenues in a residential service company? It is highly unlikely.

However, you need to have adequate cash flow to cover unexpected items that arise without disrupting your current monthly expenses. There are several ways to accumulate cash reserves and one of these can also be protected from annual taxes.

1 - Accumulate your monthly maintenance club fees in a separate account. The IRS does not require you to pay taxes on these funds until you move them into your operating budget. Once you move the funds into the general account, you will then pay them out to the technicians who performed the maintenance, in essence the revenue will be a wash with no profits incurred.

2 - The remaining funds in the maintenance account can be used to cover "discounts" that are given to club members when they purchase new equipment, in which case they would be taxable.

3 - The maintenance account can also be used to meet your financial obligations in a slow month when revenues do not match expenses.

You have likely heard the expression, "Cash is King!". Well in the case of a residential service company, this is true. You need operating cash to keep the business running.

You will want to minimize any commercial accounts that take longer than 30 days to pay you. Many business owners convince themselves they need to take this kind of work, but they fail to recognize the true cost of not getting paid right away and accumulating a large account of receivables.

You see, your expenses accrue interest when you cannot pay them off every month. This interest directly reduces the profitability of any receivables. In addition, when you do not get paid for receivables, this reduces the profits of your other work by 100% of the amount of the receivables that are not paid.

Since commercial work is often highly competitive on pricing, thus offering lower margins, it can be a risky venture. Can you see how quickly you can lose out if commercial services are not paid within 30 days?

Make sure you have money in the bank. Work hard to pay off all your debts and loans. In other words, AS MUCH AS POSSIBLE, OWN EVERYTHING!

Takeaways from this chapter.

- *Systems and solid strategies produce better results on a consistent basis.*

- *Profits are more important than revenues.*

- *You are in the marketing business.*

- *Sustained growth is never by accident.*

- *Steady growth is the best growth.*

- *A healthy business is based on service customers.*

- *A debt-free business is more profitable.*

- *Never fear paying taxes because you made a healthy profit.*

Afterword

I want to say "THANK YOU" for the service you provide! You have protected my family and friends for decades along with the millions of other homeowners in our nation. You are the silent heroes of our country who do your work without fanfare and often without the appreciation you deserve. I am your personal cheerleader and am doing my best to spread the word about the value and importance of the services you provide.

YOU and your team of employees are truly the "heartbeat" of our nation. We need for your business to thrive and to be a healthy company. Your services are necessary for us to sustain our standard of living and to maintain our status as one of the leading global citizens.

Why do I say this? Do you realize that without clean water, effective sewage transfer, dependable electricity, and refrigeration our nation would become a 3rd world country in less than a year? As a residential service business owner, you literally stand in the gap. You protect our community and society from living in chaos, filth, and disease.

The goal is to provide you with a plan and a strategy system to protect your business and take good care of your family. May you go forth and be more effective and more profitable. You deserve all the good things that come your way.

Final Note:

Thank you for reading this book. I hope it helps to clarify your thinking and your personal resolve to build a stronger, profitable business. Hopefully, this book has provided you with plenty of insights and ideas for maximizing your profits and minimizing your risks. I am here to support your success in any way that I can.

If you have a desire to contact me, it would be my pleasure to help you grow your business. I promise to return your call or email personally if possible. Either one of my colleagues or I will be happy to talk with you.

CONTACT INFORMATION:

Kerry S. Webb, PhD
CCO and President
Peak Leadership Consulting

Solutions@peakleadership.com

You may contact Dr. Kerry Webb via email for free handouts with Business KPIs for various trades, Hybrid Pay, Pricing Models, Interview Guides, Interview Scoring Sheets, and other tools mentioned in this book.

CONSULTING, COACHING, & TRAINING SERVICES:

- Sales & Growth Strategies
- Financial Strategic Planning
- Business & Sales Coaching
- Customer Service Training
- Customized Training Programs
- Homeowner Market Focus
- Company Culture
- Business Growth Solutions

www.ingramcontent.com/pod-product-compliance
Lightning Source LLC
Chambersburg PA
CBHW020657220526

45464CB00001B/468